NED ROREM

An Absolute Gift

A NEW DIARY

SIMON AND SCHUSTER · NEW YORK

Designed by Elizabeth Woll
Manufactured in the United States of America

1   2   3   4   5   6   7   8   9   10

Library of Congress Cataloging in Publication Data

Rorem, Ned, date.
    An absolute gift.

    Includes index.
    1. Rorem, Ned, 1923–   2.   Composers—United
States—Biography. I.   Title.
ML410.R693A25   780'.92'4 [B]   77-18512
ISBN 0-671-22666-5

Contents

Part Three

Part Four

To James Holmes

De nouveau et toujours le soutien et la source . . .

Foreword

These pieces are the latest in a series about so-called creative concerns. The series was begun partly as an antidote to a random diary (itself a distraction from the composer's full-time job), partly as a result of periodical invitations.

Yet as it happens the article called "Lies" is culled from the ongoing diary, while "Why I Write as I Do" was spoken at a meeting of The American Music Center, January 1974. "Pulitzer" is a batch of questions-and-answers jotted while waiting for interviewer John Gruen of *The New York Times*, May 1976. The notes for "Criticism," like those for "Vocabulary" (which first appeared in *Christopher Street*), are again from the diary, and so are the "Notes on Death."

"Our Music Now," written for the *New Republic*, is both a comment on the general state of American music and on the specific musical season of 1974. "A Cultured Winter" surveys the following season when Channel 13 experimented with a Critics Roundtable. Every fortnight Jack Richardson, Alexander Cockburn and I gathered for thirty minutes to discuss matters artistic with our host, Harold Hayes. Richardson would do a solo about a recent play (sometimes a book), Cockburn would usually review a movie, and I would criticize some concert or passing opera. After these preambles we performed as a trio, since presumably we had attended each other's "events" and were of catholic disposition. My notes were scribbled just before the broadcasts, then discarded while I "improvised." In the normal course of things I seldom hear music publicly anymore, and never go to plays. But that year, while so uncommonly active, I learned, if nothing else, that not being up-to-date was unrelated to being old hat.

The idea for reviewing Tennessee Williams' stories came from Midge Decter (on behalf of the *Saturday Review* in 1974), no doubt because she knew I had once composed scores for Williams' plays and therefore must have an angle. "Song" appeared in *The New York Sunday Times*, April 1975, and "Bagázh" in the same paper the next December. The write-up of the Metropolitan's production of Britten's *Death in Venice* was for the *New Republic*, December 1974.

Commentary published "Ravel" on the occasion of that composer's hundredth birthday. *Opera News* published "Poulenc" on the occasion of that composer's *Dialogues of the Carmelites*' being posthumously mounted at the Met. "Ezra Pound as Musician" was written eleven years ago as a preface to a reprint of a treatise by Pound.

N. R., 1978

From Life to Art by painstaking adaption
Relying on us to cover the rift;
Only your notes are pure contraption,
Only your song is an absolute gift.

"The Composer," W. H. Auden

An Absolute Gift
A NEW DIARY

Part One

1·Why I Write as I Do

What can be told about music that the music itself can't tell? Only how it came to be written.

It is instructive to hear what one composer says about another because, no matter how biased, he quite knows what he's talking about. It is less instructive to hear what a composer says about himself because, no matter how sincere, he doesn't quite know what he's talking about. A composer can clarify his method to others, but not his esthetic. He can tell how he wrote his piece, but not why. His why *is* the piece. All else is a smokescreen through which he explains what you're supposed to hear rather than what you do hear. Unless the smokescreen itself is his music.

A smokescreen is handy but fragile. Let me show you mine—which may blow away even while I'm talking.

Why do I compose the way I do?
What way is that? As with affairs of the heart each time

is the first time, and the way of a new composition is no more predictable than the way of true love. Rules observed last time must be broken this time; vices become virtues in a different setting.

Years later, when one or another of his "ways" has faded from public awareness, a composer himself finds it hard to revive the old flame, nor can he explain why the spark did or did not flare into fireworks. Of course, experience eventually teaches him how to play with fire. And it teaches him not to push comparisons: Love, even love for music, is never logical, while music, even music that inspires love, is always logical.

Why do I compose the way I do?

How answer, unless I know the effect the music has on others? That effect can never really be known, least of all while composing. While composing I can only know the effect I want to project.

No artist hopes, or even seeks, to be understood. In his heart he feels understanding to be a bit insulting: he is too complex, too special, and anyway understanding is no urgent ingredient of art as it is of more critical expressions. What he hopes for is: not to be misunderstood. For an artist, the height of misunderstanding is to be taken for clothed when in fact he is naked, to be praised for finery he has no intention of wearing.

For example. My early emigration to France was not that of an American in need of a change; I had felt myself born out of context and wanted to go back to a different womb. When I first played my pieces for my new countrymen I experienced relief and elation to be finally spilling forth my oh-so-sensual Gallic wit to comprehending ears. Now, their reaction was: Why so cold and humorless, Ned, so Nordic and inhibited? Be more French.

Do I then compose because of influences?

We all compose, probably, "through" the first music which attracted us. That music in turn was heard through music we already knew. Because I knew Ravel before Bach, I still hear Bach as I hear Ravel: those baroque sequences become static ninth chords. Because I knew French music before German, I still hear (and judge) German music as French. I still hear twelve-tone music as tonal, and still hear my own jagged airs as mere nursery exercises for blues singers. We all grow by taking from our predecessors. To refuse to take from them is itself a taking—an affirmation. The difference between a true and false artist is the difference between a conscious and an unconscious thief. The professional disguises a theft by stamping it with his trademark. The amateur has no trademark; he doesn't know he's stolen; he peddles black-and-white reproductions.

A trademark can be a speech defect. It makes no sense to disqualify a speech defect, or even a language. Criticize only what is said in the language, and despite the defect (which may be engaging). I speak my native tongue as I can. Do you hear? Will you listen? Do I hold your interest?

Aware of those I've robbed, I smile when others don't recognize them. Yet I make no claims to novelty. My sole originality is that I've never sought originality. Though in the end that claim cannot apply to my music, only to a point of view about my music.

Do I compose because I've been encouraged? Been so often singled out as a unique melodist?

I'm not a unique melodist. I am a setter of literature, which has no special claim to tunes. Any uniqueness springs from an unactive competition—at least in the domain of recital song. Every composer worthy of the name is essentially a vocal composer, be his medium a quintet of horns, a percussion ensemble, an electronic synthesizer. He is a setter of literature which makes no special claim to words. Inasmuch as I've been—against my will—pigeonholed as a songwriter I have, yes, been encouraged. Without the practicalities of praise and performance day after day, I would have given up long ago. And each day is still touch and go. Admittedly there is a professional paradox here. Although others who *know*, because their ideas are published, say my reputation is that of a song composer, of the ample variety of commissions offered me over the past ten years none have been for songs.

My three mottos for songwriting: Use only good poems— that is, convincing marvels in English of all periods. Write gracefully for the voice—that is, make the voice line as seen on paper have the arched flow which singers like to interpret. Use no trick beyond the biggest trick—that is, since singing is already such artifice, never repeat words arbitrarily, much less ask the voice to groan, shriek, or rasp. I have nothing against special effects; they are just not in my language. I betray the poet by framing his words, not by distorting them.

Why do I compose? Less from self-expression than because I want to be an audience to something that will satisfy me. The act dispels the smokescreen between my ego and reality. However my gifts may seem a luxury to others, I compose for my own necessity, because no one else makes quite the sound I wish to hear.

2· *Lies*
NOTES ON CRAFT

One

My work is my truth. Insofar as that work is also art it is also true for you. That that art may lie makes it no less true. A symbol posing as the real thing betrays itself, yet the betrayal can't disqualify the symbol's status as symbol.

That painting there's not true to life, it's scarcely true to paint. That tune's not natural, not birdsong, not wind's sough, it's false to outdoors. It sounds like nothing else. It lies.

According to who's listening we all are liars. Artists' fables are worth attending. Lies of art ring true.

Am I incapable of truth because I don't know what it is? Whatever truth may be, it's not the opposite of lie. In art it is that which can be cared about, that which we believe.

Those who say, "Look out, he'll quote you in that diary," are the very ones I never notice. The others, they're safe, they can't win, I don't quote, I misquote. Lurking behind the exquisite monster, I'm capable of guidance—that is, of guiding him. The matriarch's mother.

Who most loathe the diary are those depicted within. What they most loathe is not precious archness, not opinions stated as facts nor the urbane reflections posing as pastorale *pensées*, but seeing their life reduced to anecdote, however crass or laudatory. "I was there," they say, "I keep a diary too, I remember what happened, and you're wrong." Of course there's no such thing as *the* truth, there is only *one's* truth, and even that fluxes with each passing hour. Though I disown nothing, I've come to value discretion, even to claim it among virtues broader than mere truth. Mere truth. Yet in the old days it never occurred to me that friends would feel hurt from my passing verities.

A book's a book, not real life. Yet when offered for real, as a diary, the book must be arranged to seem real. The very arranging teaches an author artifices of life itself, outgrowths which in the telling become more natural than in their larval stage of mere being.

It means nothing that I can't understand John Ashbery's poetry, because I can't understand any poetry. Oh, occasionally after making a song from a poem I may intuit some vague message in the words, through the music—although, of course, the music means nothing either.

All true artists are modest but try not to show it.

(No true artists are modest but they pretend to be?)

Common to all greatness is the sense of vulnerability, and the keynote to greatness is less genius than patience.

Was *Rashomon* three versions of a lie, or of a truth? Are diaries less honest inherently than novels?

Diaries are a sideline, notebooks wherein a person records problems of work and play. Nearly always, though, they are kept with the intention of being read; so like all art they dissimulate by becoming a code. The diarist doesn't present himself, but an idea of himself, and only that idea of himself which he chooses to publicize.

As a literary form the diary is hardly new (it's far older than the novel) except as an indigenous American utterance, public confession not having been our bent until recently. Yet confession risks adopting the features of the very mask novelists hide behind. Our century's best-known diarist, André Gide, during the blitzes of World War Two, blissfully notated adventures with Arab lads in his Biskra retreat. To tell it like it is is no more a property of diaries than of fiction. Lives are not facts, nor does the present moment exist; an author can necessarily record the present only after the fact. Of itself truth is not persuasive; even less is it art. And who, including the diarist himself, can prove that the character represented is, in this guise, finally, the *real* author? Does Baudelaire's journal disclose more to us of Baudelaire than Genet's novels do of Genet? Could Philip Roth have composed his complaint in another form without its becoming more rather than less of a mask? To fictionalize the real makes it easier to be honest. The realist novel of the thirties became the unrealistic autobiography of the sixties. Still, all real works of art (be they geometric sculptures, children's poetry, or reports on Hanoi) speak to us, by definition, with their creator's voice.

A voice is a voice, unfakeable. We cannot lie, no matter what tone we pretend to—or in fact *do*—project, no matter how we try to shade or disguise that voice, no matter what master's words or songs we filch and, like reverse dybbuks, sing through our own lips. No one can lie, the body cannot lie, and the wiliest plagiarism is verifiable. What is not verifiable is why those fingerprints are more amusing than these, or why some standard stolen goods take on a wilder luster on a thief's back. Alas, most thefts are of trash and remain trash.

The difference between a journalist and a diarist is that one reports what happened, the other reports a reaction to what happened. Yet both are susceptible to cries of liar. Rightly. Less truthful than a painter, a photographer *is* bias: a camera selects the angle and snaps its subject unawares, especially if the subject is a tree. The tree is a lie, but not the picture of it. If truth is fact, then all art—which only represents fact, and one person's version of that—lies, but by extension speaks true.

After four sittings Alvin Ross has finished his second portrait of me, thirty years to the hour after the first one (now lost) in Philadelphia in 1943. It looks exactly like me, but not at all like me.

Two weeks ago Alvin bought at the A&P a marble cake which he plans to paint for his dessert series. Today the cake, far from having decayed, has turned, thanks to preservatives, into solid marble.

Talent to the talented holds no wonder. It is a duty, even a burden, like going to the outhouse or milking the goats. Joy, especially early joy, springs from the talent of others, their books, their songs.

He has spent his whole life in Chartres. Only at twenty did he learn that not every town in the world harbored a big church. That his big church was special never occurred to him. But that children in America or China did not realize their lack of a big church was frightening.

Deaths today by cancer and by murder, of Lily Pons and Sal Mineo. This famous pair led starlit lives and were, as the saying goes, appreciated; their very nonanonymity is healthy if only by bringing to public light (starlight?) their unhealthy finales. Yet they were only interpreters, so what have they left—that is, left to us? Works of art they performed were at best second-class. It is, of course, bromidic to ask what does anyone finally leave, yet I ask it hourly.

JH confides he's been glancing through some of my notes, and hopes, should they ever be published, that I'll delete a reflection about his voice sounding sad on the phone. Now, I'm as responsive to the desires of JH as to those of any living person, but it is a diarist's nature to include precisely what others would have him exclude. There lies the danger. Estrangements don't come from what people find gossipy about other people, but from what they find incomplete— and thus untrue—about themselves, for truth means only the whole truth. Indeed, for me to read what's written about me is to see a life reduced to several lines—sometimes ecstatic, sometimes sarcastic—and to find myself miniaturized and existing for others who, because they see fractionally, find me peripheral to their own laws. In a diary no mention of a person can be, to that person, the *right* mention, since no mention of anything (even of E equals mc squared) is all-inclusive, and so can be only a lie. My own mention of others, even of myself, means to me only what it means during the moment of mention, since we change pores—natures, reality—with each fluid second.

What is comparatively stable is the sadness of JH's voice on the phone. If this were all that signified to me I would (at his request) omit mention of it, as wrongly I have omitted whimsies or eccentricities or passing "perversions," at their request, of others, thereby diluting the blood—the *truth, my* truth, however superficial—of the published diary in the past, because the diary became no longer a biased

monologue but a fair exchange. If I mention the sadness of
JH's voice it's because I am so vulnerable to the sound; in
fact my susceptibility is such that, when we met a decade
ago, I understood that for the remainder of my life another
person would never fill his special shoes, and that I could
(and largely did) renounce a certain sociability without feeling anything but richer. JH is everything, and to write that
is to compromise us both far more than any mention of a
sad voice. Should he choose that I also delete this paragraph,
I shall. Though where then will be my documented verities,
fragmented but contradictorily (if only through style),
flowing, continual, and in a way necessary because inimitable?

Art moves us, propaganda changes us. Art takes us in a
circle, propaganda in a straight line. Art collides with propaganda, producing a tantrum to attract the grownups who,
being no less childlike than the artists, take it as a game, a
game without rules that goes on forever, or at least—as in
medieval oubliettes—until death.

Circling the square. Let the music flutter like leaves, be
passive to the wind, assume a "natural" shape (which
throughout the universe is circular) rather than the forced
angles of art. Circling the square: cruising outside the central marketplace.

Freudian slips of the tongue would hold more interest if
they were less just that: casual slips, a foot's accidental ex-
cursion into a puddle, which is not really so foreign an
environment for feet. Sound-alikes are too predictably the
result of fatigue or embarrassment, or of man's penchant for
rhyme, for building on a given: mercy for merry, sorrow
queen for sour cream, sew me to a sheet for show me to a

seat, maybe money for honey. To call your present lover by the name of a previous lover is not so rare. Give me someone who unexpectedly says butterfly for oatmeal, says ambergris for confidential, yes for when, peach for swan, or who, at twenty and for the first time ever, calls his father mother.

"Seeing that artists tend to make good the year after they die," wrote Paul Goodman, "an artist gives out that he is dead and vanishes. Nothing happens. Twenty years later, in Mexico, he in fact dies, and the year following he makes good."

Yes, but a dozen others die and don't make good. And what about the poor suicide who, a day later, is quite forgotten, and for twenty years and forever? If in fact (though it is no fact) unknown artists tend to make good a year after they die, known artists tend to fade away. For every Plath or Bartók who burst out, a Gide or a Hindemith is not long mourned. What of Paul himself? Was his sudden fame at fifty a sort of death from which he was resurrected (since when he did die at sixty-one he was again comparatively forsaken)? Today where is he? For if friends who count do recall, others don't, and friends aren't what Paul would have meant by making good.

Vancouver. So much traveling, yet never blasé toward planes. Those brief hours, from Manhattan to this far shore of Canada, sailing over America (where there still are, as Gertrude said, "more people where nobody is than where anybody is") demand conjecture. The months it took an early settler! From a valley he saw one mountain, from its peak another mountain, again into the valley, and so on, forever, waves blanked out the future. But we watch that future—that spatial future—from above, before it exists for the landbound. If in fact there is a spatial future, is there not, too, a temporal future, preexisting like a fan before it's opened? If so, when opened, can we perceive beyond the ridge which is our death?—not to discover if there's life after death, but to discover if there's life after *our* life? I'm confusing time and space; a plane does move in time as it covers space. What about a helicopter, hovering motionless above a clear view of both spatial and temporal future? Still, the future does not exist. If the future existed, it would not, by definition, be the future.

Perspective depends on your mood of the hour. Monday my host came to the hotel to tape an interview. For two hours I answered fourteen carefully prepared questions. The tape was lost. Tuesday morning I agreed to retape the interview. To the same fourteen questions I gave new answers. Both sets of answers were honest, but on Tuesday I was a different person. I was a different person less by being a day older than by having exhausted a viewpoint, or at least my examples of viewpoint. Now, if the original interview had occurred Tuesday it could have been the same as on Monday (despite snow which had fallen overnight) because the questions would be hitting me for the first time. On the other hand, had the second tape been also lost and a third identical interview been set up for Wednesday, I would have refused. By Wednesday I would have turned into a teacher. Teachers repeat themselves.

Students don't learn by instruction but by imitation.

Teaching means: to lead a horse to water and to make him drink. A teacher takes joy in other people's self-discovery. An artist takes joy in other people's joy at *his* self-discovery, a joy so acute it is edged in a pain which adds to its value like goldplate on silver. Teachers know, artists do. Obviously the two can overlap. Myself, I've not a Socratic bone in my body.

You can't teach a young dog old tricks. (Ironically, some young dogs are older than me. Among my crop at Utah were those whose idea of the ultimate was to set the words of Brigham Young to music.) Young composers aren't that interested in the past.

Of course a trick is by definition new. When it's old it's a rule.

Nantucket style. A Mrs. Winthrop, who has a TV show, inquires about "personalities" she might interview. I tell her that, except she's gone, Francine du Plessix Gray would have been perfect.

"Who?" asks Mrs. Winthrop.

"Francine Gray, a journalist and religionist who's about to publish her first novel which is already a Book-of-the-Month selection. She worked here all during August with her husband Cleve, the painter, and their two sons, in a house they rented on Mill Street."

"I love Mill Street," says Mrs. Winthrop.

In the post office up comes a Mrs. Jordan, big cheese on the committee of Nantucket's summer concert series. Without stopping she poses three unanswerable questions: "And what have you been doing?" (Suffering from piles, *ma bonne*, and making cakes, talking to strangers.) "Writing lots of beautiful music for us?" (For you? How much of that beautiful music do you already know, and are you willing to pay?) "Doesn't our summer's series look divine?" (But since there's no American piece on any of the six recitals during this Bicentennial year, how can I care?)

Suppose I expressed myself aloud? Far from taking offense, she would take pity, arrange to have me asked to participate, which I would refuse, so feelings would harden.

At a dinner party sans style a Mrs. Malingo (Floridian and affluent) declares that *The New York Times* has "crucified" Nixon. Without malice I say, "I've heard about people like you but never actually met one." She regards me warily, never having met one of me either, and literally holds back the tears.

Full time and willy-nilly do I chase two careers never knowing quite if their mutual infringement is harmful or fruitful. To spill out verbs instead of notes should disquiet me. Yet this prose is a sieve: What oozes through is rarefied, becomes distilled and turns to "abstract" sound on staves. Is whatever clogs the meshes scraped out and smeared undiluted onto diary paper?

How can I know if my prose and music interfere with each other? Without the prose would the music be better or just thicker? Without the music would there be a subject for the prose?

Only as a composer am I qualified to soliloquize, since my life is no longer amorous, voluble, or drunk, and since I've no more friends—certainly no new ones (who would they be? and what could they bring that I couldn't find in their works?—except a taxi to the hospital in moments of need, moments, however, growing paradoxically fewer as one gets feebler). Killing time. Now that I am allowed to speak, have I more to say?

Yet what's useless? At fifty one's perspective demonstrates that time's logic is contrary to the logic of space. The future shrinks as we approach, while the past, receding, expands. The expanse changes meaning daily through the knowledge that our remaining number of heartbeats grows always fewer like a speedometer being rewound—that is, wound back, but never to be started again.

Apparently I state with some succinctness on the art of others, putting a steady finger on how the method provokes rise or fall. What of my own art? Have I principles by which to proceed? Often noted here are comments that I'm composing this or that, or that that or this was premiered here or there (comments quaintly satirized by Howard Moss). But what I preach, or even practice, is best shown verbally in what I say of others. To explain that music must speak for itself is a lame out, since every artist, whatever he may admit, has both a technical and moral angle about the language he chooses to utter.

A diary—a public diary—is no more spontaneously composed than a symphony. Yes, themes may come all of a piece from the impulsive and recalcitrant muse, but they are set in gold alone, or sewn together, and forever revised before they are printed. That the expressive (the artistic, if you will) process can be untampered with is fallacy. Abandon takes rehearsal. Sometimes a song, a paragraph (like this one) emerges effortlessly. However it springs forth, art must seem seamless.

The hero of my diary is a fictional man upon whom I've worked hard but who has little to do with me—including the me penning this sentence, who is also the hero of my diary.

Two

Music's the grandest lie. Music's not reality but a representation of one aspect of fact which in turn is but one aspect of truth. Possibly truth has no needed tie to fact. In which case, yes, truth approaches music (or vice versa) but only in that generalized befuddled Polonius-Keats equation of truth and beauty.

Friends never complain that they have been misrepresented in my music. Have they, indeed, been represented? Even the composer cannot say.

Persuasiveness of harmony. Harmony fixes mood more than do tune or rhythm. Thus it's Chopin, or 1930s swing, with the rapid shifting of regular secondary sevenths, that most moves me. . . . To no poet am I drawn more than to Goodman, to no painter more than to Vuillard, to no human visages more than to Belmondo's or Vitti's. No pastry's more tempting than warm pear tarts, no sonic formula more satisfying than Bach's sequences, no ambience more conclusive than a verdant cloister, and no time of day more pregnant than twilight if I'm not alone. No danger thwarts more than the past, no fragrance exalts more than winter chestnuts (though I loathe any odor of body, perfumed or natural, even of youth, which once I praised).

Beauty outlasts youth. Beauty's tougher than. Sex increasingly repels—the smell of it. To grow old is to climb higher and higher through branches which become scarcer, brittler. Almost alone up there one does see clearly far and wide and behind and beneath. But the seeing contains no understanding, nor is there much to look at, nothing to compel the gaze.

Someday formulate an answer to the oft-asked but fair question, "Does your mood affect your composition?" (The question's as fertile as "What makes a good poem for music?" Depends on kind of music, requirements of singer, etc.) The answer: I don't know, outsiders must judge. Definitions of happy and sad music change with the generations, and a composer at his happiest might pen his sad refrains. Does he compose according to how he feels today, to how he feels in general, or in delayed reaction to how he felt last year or as a child? He composes less according to transient states than to the needs of the piece, which takes on a life of its own once under way. Personal mood depends on flow of time, but when a composer's composing his woes and joys are suspended and time jells.

The Diabelli Variations: a magic mountain from a molehill.

People need formulas. They ask, "When do you work?" hoping to learn that composers put pen to paper each morning at seven and go on till tea. Now, by the time composers put pen to paper the composing is done; this is the inscription of the act, not the act itself.

Never say "I'm working well"; it brings bad luck. The nightmare—or rather, nightmare's sibling—which composers know too well: insomnia forcing them through the wee hours to jot notes which next morning ring false.

The sorry postponement of writing it down, writing it down . . . because when written down it might not be good enough. Such intellectual trepidation is, if you will, uncreative —and I say "intellectual" advisedly: the intelligence of certain composers impedes them from simply making it up as it goes along. Rule of thumb: Compose first, worry later. Or: Speak before you think and write it down afterwards. Actually all composers think before they speak. The speaking is the writing down.

Which came first, the punishment or the crime? Was the Inquisition concocted to legitimize the pleasures of torture?

Are cruel acts, committed in the name of the Lord or for the good of the people, ever honestly meant for the good of the people or in the name of the Lord? Which came first, law-breaker or law? In music, of course, rules came after the fact, to substantiate (to justify, *excuse*) what composers made up as they went along. Let a piece flow out, then think up reasons for the flow. Yet what teacher could thus counsel a student? Though precisely the reverse is strait-jacketing: to fear the flow because of reasons coming before the flow.

Composers' secrets? Some love to tell secrets of how a piece is made. It shouldn't be how, but how well. Describe form, and form is all a hearer hears. Then observe that fugue of Bach, crystalline, with friendly head or heads intermittently popping forth from the tangles. Tangles? No, tails continually attached. Friends in tangled tails, crystalline, which need not be sliced like Medusa's curls or the Gordian knot, for at the end the tails grow heads again, codas, stretti, logical hoorays.

I am never *not* working, yet I never catch myself in the act. At the end of each year I've somehow produced around an hour of music, and that hour is not a few sheets of penciled whole notes, but hundreds of pages of inked orchestration. Work is the process of composing—making it up as it goes along, which is the only precise description since Homer. The action is at once so disparate and so compact that the actor is unaware, which is doubtless why I "never find myself" etc. I don't consider as work the post-compositional drudgery (often pleasant) of copying, instrumentation, rehearsal, letter-writing, or dealing with publishers, though all this is time-consuming. Nor do I consider as work the compiling of my books, which is the assembling of pre-written fragments. I do consider as work the answering of this question: "When do you work?"—since it concerns, like musical composition, the placement of notion into order. As to when, and is it daily, I notate when I have a commissioned deadline and don't when I don't: the goal is functional, and its approach makes me scribble ten hours a day. Between commissions months are eaten looking at soap operas.

It's been decades since I've worked with the youthful Need to Express Myself. What I *do* express today is finer wrought and aims higher than yesterday although it might not ring truer. Our gifts are not gifts, but paid for terribly. Work is not play. The crunching responsibility forces many to throw in the sponge at the height of glory. Would they have persisted so long without encouragement?

I am able to postpone indefinitely the notation of a composition on the senseless rationale that, once written, it can never *become* written. With equal reason, I cannot complete a composition without feeling, well, there's one more piece chalked up before I die.

When do I work? Continually. Anyone's ego brings all to himself, leaves nothing for others, like pollen for bees. The ultimate honey isn't consciously manufactured to delight. When work? Between the lines of the soap opera I forever sift for useful matter. But I do work also to reconstruct the alchemy which fired those early songs which were sometimes of real gold, and which paradoxically had no formula beyond the one given by a hand which as easily took it away.

Every piece is the first. Over the years we learn to put notes mechanically together, yet the blank page remains no less terrifying than for a blocked beginner.

Stage fright. Each time's the first. If over the years I'm geared to play better in public than in private, I'm no less anxious before going to the lions. Still, to be on stage is exhilarating as sex: I do the work, but *they* are making me do it—they are not passive at all.

Of course, I'm never on stage except as pianist for my own songs. If something goes wrong, who's responsible? To sit impotently in the audience while the songs are massacred up there is the ultimate torment; the composer is held responsible for the singer's unwitting sabotage. I'd rather make my own music than hear it, even played well.

My musical memory is visual. Should the muse approach incongruously—on the subway, in a steam bath—and find me without a notebook, I will quickly picture in my mind the five strands of a staff, snatch from the air the inspiring notes glittering like bats, glue them to the staff, take a snapshot with an imaginary camera and, reaching home, develop the film on actual paper. The result is usually worthwhile, more so than similar transactions in dreams which next morning turn out to be trash. The music of night is unworked-for, untrue; true music, transmittable music, true ease, is difficult.

Back from six days in Iowa and South Dakota where on two successive nights the oratorio *Little Prayers* was premiered. Except for the soloists (Irene Gubrud and William Powers), the performance forces were unduplicated, Trautwein conducting the Sioux Falls Orchestra and a chorus of three hundred on Saturday, and Kucinski leading the Sioux City Symphony and a quite different chorus on Sunday. Previous to these occasions I lectured in widely spaced centers (including the Yankton of my childhood), mornings, afternoons, evenings, and managed to come through without once failing my regulated toilet habits. This region of the Middle West is a latticework of maternal Millers and of

Rorems, of Republicans, real Indians on street corners, and lots of homemade pies.

After each rehearsal they thank me for "sparing the time" to give suggestions. Quaint reaction. Of course, since they've never met a composer before, they çan't realize that he has more to lose than they by an unprepared performance. But "sparing the time" from what? From work? This *is* my work. From a charismatic life? That life exists only because I occasionally spare time from work for it. (I don't occasionally spare time from parties so as to write a symphony.)

Glamour and temperament, the supposed attributes of a star, are luxury items reserved for the intermission. No true artist—no Auden, say, or Callas—brings a "difficult" side to the scene of work except sometimes as priority to speed up matters; a demanding artist, if he's an artist, is always correct in his demands. Only nonprofessionals bring glamour to rehearsals.

For years I've been lamenting at universities the ignorance of their students. "How," I declare, "can a musician call himself that who doesn't know *Le Sacre* by heart?" Suddenly I realized that my moth-eaten score of the masterwork (which I, age twelve, stole from Lyon & Healy's) had long since vanished. I bought a new copy and went to bed with it last night. How clean, how Haydnesque *Le Sacre* looks now, with no note superfluous, no pattern complex, no color dirty, no formal section particularly difficult anymore.

"What do you consider your most important education?"
"Self-taught."
"But we've read you had a Master's from Juilliard."
"So I have. I'd quite forgotten."
For a full degree at Juilliard one took nonmusical courses. Having passed the entrance exams with flying colors, I

wasn't required to attend musical classes except in piano and composition. What I therefore recall most clearly of that illustrious school in 1946–48 are studies in sociology, American history, physical education and, yes, hygiene (which taught that the human diet needs copper as well as iron, copper being obtained both through apricots and through milk stored in brass vats). Also two semesters of world literature which, if nothing else, did inspire some musical output including songs on texts both sacred and profane, notably *Four Madrigals* to Sappho fragments.

What genius! one hears of the soloist during an intermission. Why genius? He doesn't invent the music, nor does he, as people say, bring it to life. Music exists always, unrendered yet breathing, even on Grecian urns. The soloist is a vessel (an urn) through which preexisting music passes. Now a vessel may be of Steuben glass or a tin can, but a vessel is not the cause of its contents. Genius is a word I don't use. If I did, I would not, surely, apply it to an interpreter. To a composer? Well, vessel is not my word either, but Stravinsky's. Questioned as to the creative process which brought his masterpiece into being, he replied, "I am merely the vessel through which *Le Sacre* flowed."

Brief chat with Stephen Sondheim all about his score for *Stavisky*, which I'd liked. That he knows neither the French language nor the craft of orchestration is eyebrow-raising, not because he's so notoriously adept at Double-Crostics (the various knacks don't overlap, nor do tastes for the various arts), but because one would suppose in him a broader curiosity. Foreign tongues are, after all, puzzles that can be solved; and orchestration is a trade, not an art: anyone can do it. A composer's unique reward is to hear his work take life, to know that all those players must join to activate his flyspecked staves whose sonorous combinations he alone has dreamed up as means of setting into relief—putting into color—his basic premise. To hear this music as "realized" by a hired arranger is surely less tantalizing than to hear it as realized by himself. Yet the more money a composer makes, the less he has concretely to do with his own élans.

Laziness is due not to too few but to too many notions, all fully realized. They aren't waiting to be born, but to be notated, and oh the drudgery, because they exist, almost complete—at least theatrically—there on the staves of the brain. The hours spent writing them down could be better spent thinking them up. Or so I reason, and get sick.

"When do you find time to compose?" people ask, assuming that to compose is a transitive verb, the action of placing notes on paper (or worse, of rambling over the keys). Time for that action is comparatively minimal: anyone finds time for any action that means anything to him. When do I do anything else? might be a better question, since in some way each breath drawn, awake or asleep, is musical; at parties, the A&P, a Turkish bath, in the Metro, reading *Lear*, I'm never not composing, will it or no. Euterpe's a healthy succubus. The action? That's merely the final boring chore.

Being a computer, I lack imagination and cannot guess at meanings, so I must *learn* languages. I have no intuition and cannot recognize music unless I already know it, so I must memorize each example of a repertory. I have no ear and cannot think up colors or tunes, so to compose music I mimic the great (like the voiceless Chaplin who sings beautifully only when imitating Caruso). I am literal-minded and thus without humor, so I must employ a programmed wisdom which shows me what is truly witty. I explain all this to Felicia, who takes it at face value and offers her condolence.

Three

People sometimes ask why I don't set my prose to music. I set words to music I feel can take a change. As a composer of songs I don't seek to improve words so much as to re-emphasize them—to alter their dimension. Music can't heighten the meaning of words, only change their meaning (unless to heighten be a form of change). Occasionally the words benefit from the change; but although they might not inherently *need* this change, I must feel that they need it.

Now, to write words with an intention of setting them would be to write words I intended by definition to change. Only a bad text could emerge from so inhibiting a task. Nor could I musicalize words I had written at another time and for their own sake, since those words would not exist if I had been able (at that other time) to express their sense in music. As for composing words and music simultaneously, that is a game for precocious children, and presupposes a third party beneath the skin of the composer-poet: the performer. Balladeers are triple personalities dealing in short forms (or repetitious narratives). The mere dual personality, or nonperforming composer-writer, usually deals in large librettos which he writes as he goes along. Menotti, Blitzstein, Tippett, Nono.

There is already a presumption in a composer who sets a poet to music. To direct this presumption toward his own prose would be presumptuousissimo.

The woman across the street (with whom I share an aversion for a little boy at the corner who rides around his front yard on a sputtering Honda) asks: "I hear you're having a piano moved in. Does that mean we'll be hearing beautiful music?"

To be overheard composing. This invasion of privacy is more anxious-making than to be surprised by a total stranger while you're on the toilet. The endless foundering of the so-called creative act is more intimate, more unrehearsed, than the surgeon's cut. Over and over and over and over again the trial and error, the error and trial, the in-directed cross-exam, the flop. How can the woman know—who is used to a finished product played by a star on a record? Yet even were I a pianist, she would pose the same question and assume that virtuosos practice inspiredly and up to tempo.

JH has been practicing too much. Practicing and learning are unrelated practices. Learning's highest intensity is in the first minutes of deciphering (or even in the first hearing) of a new piece. Once learned, the only reason for practicing is not so that the piece will get better, but so that it won't get worse.

Once learned, pieces don't get better with practice, though they can get different, and sometimes stale. (I don't swallow Casals' claim that he found newness in Bach each day of his life. With everything new we find, we lose something old.) Practicing is so that, even if your performance is at its worst, it will be up to your own minimum standards.

Awakened with, still flowing through remembered dreams, Debussy's ever-friendly Trio Sonata. The first movement unmistakably represents quails mating. In these four measures preceding ⬚1 and the seven preceding ⬚5 a female flute preens serenely among flecks of grain in the gravel, while the stupid male viola struts roughing his ruff. And that harp? Well, the harp's the garden path up and down which they walk making patterns for Amy Lowell whom I've not thought of in decades, but mightn't she have composed those verses during the very months Debussy composed his?

The most sadly seductive key change in all literature is at [20]. How carefully the composer, during the five preceding measures, prepares his "unprepared" modulation.

"What a waste of time," I sigh, as the players put down their bows after a performance of Mendelssohn's Quintet, and the hall goes wild. A woman in front of us turns with hot contempt: "You think you can do better?" What does she mean? Better at what? At playing, at composing? No, I couldn't do better, I couldn't do at all. I can't play a fiddle, and I sing a different language from the precocious Mendelssohn. But is the woman there because she can't do as well? Is music's purpose to show us how unexcellent we are? Or are we merely to "experience" music? In which case, if the experience doesn't catch fire, must we keep quiet? Oh, the sacrosanct ordinariness of these Classical Concert reactions!

People suggest that I sneer at musical masterpieces. It's not a sneer, it's awe taken for granted. I won't deny the fact of masterpieces (though some are my cup of tea while others are straight medicine). We are preconditioned to this one, another we "discover," but both kinds, once swallowed, can't stay with us daily, or we'd have time for nothing else—for searching out new masterpieces, maybe composing one ourselves. Since rarely now I sit down and listen to, say, Beethoven's Fifth, the very rareness permits fresh surprise: Why, it *is* marvelous! despite the fact that we *know* it's marvelous.

That symphony's marvelousness is self-contained. In a so-called collaborative venture conclusions are less black and white. I never hear Stravinsky's *Oedipus Rex*, for instance, without the uneasy feeling that the ancient drama more than the music is what makes it tick. Indeed, Sophocles' specter haunts and finally crushes all intruders in his dust. Not Racine nor Gide nor Cocteau nor Stravinsky nor even Freud, while in the shadow of the Greek master, remains more than a dabbler with the Oedipian hangup.

As to that hangup (the now unrefuted fact of which has shaped and shaded our century), is it too soon to admit I was never persuaded? An appealing conundrum, it still did not apply to me who cherished my father. The Oedipus hangup was another of Freud's poems, fallacious as the age-old notion of female fallibility.

Finished a little song based on Jean Garrigue's *Where We Came*, not for myself but for the memorial program Ben Weber is organizing. Now, although I admired Jean's poems (without especially liking them), would I on my own have thought of setting one? Can I yet know if the result is good? A song is as good as the vitality invested by singer and audience, and has nothing to do with its composer's inspiration. Some of my "realest" songs have been deemed bloodless by best friends.

Barbarity of refinement, ugliness of dinner parties. Words issuing from, as food enters, wet mouths. (Barbarians, in fact, move apart to eat.) Heredity and environment are one.

Ponderous snow, ponderous sunshine, the world crumbles and everything seems to hurt—poor nations, rich Americans, the tomato in the lunch pail, even the rocks. To sympathize and be of no help, there is no help. I'm not the person JH invents for himself. But if not, do I then exist? Can others become those we construct from need, if that need changes daily? Do we invent ourselves as well? If so, do the molecules of our work—our "product"—remain more stationary, more intact, than we do? A Chopin nocturne is more real than Chopin, but its reality exists in as many versions as there are people to hear it, and each version alters with each performance.

Any lie contains some truth by the fact of being uttered.

No one asks, "Do you think your songs lack strength?" unless he feels those songs lack strength. To think it (though the thought may be in but one head) means that somewhere the songs do lack strength—strength for whatever strength means (since strength is not all force and muscle). Strength means spine. *Placet futile* is stronger than all the sound and fury of *Harold in Italy*.

Would I stand up for what I believe? What do I believe? Not, certainly, generalities, homeland or God or one genre of music locking antlers with another. I do believe in my work (although faith in that work hangs by a thread), and, maybe, in my many loves. But manifestation, proselytization, a raised voice, I shy from, and it's not just Midwestern boyishness. The *en masse* shriek at Chicago football games was always meaningless. Overt enthusiasm or defiance—re art or Israel or ESP—strikes me as common. Yet I'm more "outward" far than JH.

I am not interested in restrictions of participation, nor in composing according to my own limitations. I chant less well than the average communicant, but my mute notions soar high. Because they confuse worthy activity with art, American choruses have a built-in amateurism that discourages a composer.

My first songs were on Psalms. It never occurred to me

that they were "appropriate" for church. I'd chosen the verses for their literary worth, not for their rapport with what Virgil Thomson calls "the Jesus Business." Trials of Job, like TV commercials, become too much of a bad thing.

I don't know much about church music from the inside (nuanced definitions of anthem vérsus hymn, breakdown of the Mass, and so forth), yet always delivered what was asked for, keeping a distance. It worked out that way.

I do know what church music is not. It is not a subdivision of a larger genre. All music is church music in that all music expresses what church music expresses: praise and despair.

Iain Hamilton, lest we fail to make the analogy, hurries to point out that his *Epitaph*, based on lines from Revelations, is "For This World and Time." If the music's not hip, the subtitle is, thereby passing the test of today's swinging clerics, updaters of the rock ritual. Now the Church is not rock, the Church is The Rock. The point of the Church is conservatism. The Church does not change with the times. For when do times change? Each decade? Each hour? Shall Billy Baldwin rethink the Vatican? To wear the latest fashion you must have the right figure.

Charles Wuorinen and I have nothing in common, not even music. Yet for a brief minute, during a composers' panel at Saint John the Divine, we exchange glances of complicity when the question of money is touched. Because as artists we want the rewards of Mammon, we become lambs for those Philistines who believe only in God.

Ask not what music can do for the Church, but what the Church can do for music. Performances are generally lousy, there's little money in it for composers, and the congregation doesn't come for the melodies. To include the parishioners by writing tunes facile enough for them is to treat music not as an art—as an end in itself for the Lord's glory—but as a

means to keep folks awake. To overemphasize audience participation is to condescend, to suppose that listening is not
participatory. It takes two to tango. Good will and an open
mind are more urgent than being able to sing (badly) the
patronizing phrases composed just for you.

It is less horrid to hear hard pieces played badly than easy
pieces played badly. Easier to fake *Funérailles* than *Le
tambourin*.

If one cannot serve both God and Mammon, I'll serve
Mammon.

"There is no God," screamed Anna de Noailles. "If God
existed, he'd have told me first of all."

The sacred and profane styles, so-called, of so many, are
indistinguishable. Wagner's *Parsifal* and *Venusberg,* Poulenc's *Mamelles* and *Stabat,* Britten's *War Requiem* and
Death in Venice are brewed from the same irrepressible perfumes. Composers speak one language only, though they can
speak it well or poorly depending on the weather. Or depending on God, who sometimes arranges that their holy
music is not "as good as" their sin tunes.

All organ music is implicitly sacred, specifically Christian.
Even such "abstract" solos as the Bach and Hindemith sonatas, the Brahms preludes or the pantheistic essays of Messiaen are religious by extension, since the organ sound is
equated by everyone with Church. Which is why so many
people hate the sound. As I was an attender of Silent Meeting, the sound entered childhood surreptitiously, yet I too
steered clear, preferring the neat economical slyness of
French musical thought to the blurred expensive obviousness
of the greasy organ hues which seem somehow German.

Now, correcting two penchants, Quakerism and music,
I've finished a set of eleven organ solos for Alice Tully and
Leonard Raver. Epigraphs from Quaker "thinkers" justify

(if justice be needed) these loud homages to the Silent Meeting.

George Fox was right about all religious shams except the biggest sham of all: the existence of God.

Organists hear differently from real people. They spend their lives in echo chambers. At organ recitals an outsider's ears (including the ears of a composer who may have written skillfully for the instrument) try plaintively to part the doubly exposed rich purple flesh of sound and to find the music's bone. For an organist the blur *is* the music.

JH is not garrulous, he speaks when there's something to say. I talk all the time, for if there's never much that needs saying, the exercise stimulates, and "communication" comes by restating what *is*. Art is redundant. JH is really more Quaker than I.

Can silence be an art? A fine art? Silence, of course, is the very yeast that makes music breathe, but silence by itself is just silence, not an art.

"Who hath wrote so much as the Quakers?" asked Francis Bugg. "He that doth not write whilst he is alive, can't speak when he is dead," answered John Bellers in the seventeenth century. Silence as craft, however, is cultivated by Quakers, not to mention Trappists.

Each new word an infant learns withdraws him further from what we call nature. The wiser our books become, the less knowledge (knowledge?) we control of sensual things; yet it's too late to learn from or even play with the deer and the antelope as though they were like us, and music—with its poor, crafty, dislocated imitations—is all there remains for humans.

What I avidly believe for years and then finally freeze into words (freezing this phrase here too) I can no longer believe avidly. Like composing a piece. Once it's composed I obviously no longer need to compose it—it's verity no longer craved. Such sloughing off of a truth leaves me hollow and scared of death until I fall upon another truth to fertilize and forsake. For there are many truths, but alas, no One Truth. Except maybe memory, a receding street, a solacing blank.

The summer stint, because ending, looks to have been good; while it lasted I've never been more anxious: continual nasal allergy aggravated continual shrieking of the kids next door, plus being trapped in heaven, growing old in both skin and travail. God knows I've never allowed that experience had much to do with what we call creativity, for artists don't need knowledge, they need artistry. (You don't have to know what makes babies to make babies.) But I've not left this small island in nineteen weeks, and all I can see is myself.

Once upon a time when a piece was finished it was finished, *assez!*, don't look back; and ah, the bored bemusement that they for whom the piece was wrought (was finished) should now be taken by it, since I was elsewhere launched! Tonight, three weeks before another birthday, I scan the summer's many pieces like the final shot in *Citizen Kane* panning over the packed-up crockery, and wonder at my inability to duplicate some of them, not because they're bad but because they're good. No thrilling costly architecture proposed by the dentist will I accept now, just let him scrape the gums some, stanch the blood. Not rest, not yet, please. But to escape from the body.

3·Pulitzer

How does it feel to win the Pulitzer? Totally satisfying. It's a once-in-a-decade refashioner carrying the decree that bitterness is henceforth unbecoming. And if you die in shame and squalor, at least you die Official. I never counted on it. Not because I felt undeserving but because academics presumably frowned on my wayward ways. That the judges should prove unbiased fills me with cheer for the Establishment. Except there is no more Establishment. Composers of every size and shape warmly phoned or wrote, though very few performers. That's because doers and makers move in quite separate professional—hence social—orbits. Players face out, composers in.

Ironically it was for an orchestral rather than for a vocal piece. My reputation, such as it is, has always centered around song, or the various tentacles of song: opera, chorus, cantata. *Air Music,* commissioned by Tommy Schippers for the Cincinnati Symphony, is a half-hour work in ten balletic sections, each of which uses smallish and unusual groups of instruments. Yet although all the sections are, as they say, abstract, in that they eschew the human voice and don't "mean" anything, I conceived them as I conceive all music, vocally. Whatever my music is written for—tuba, tambourine, tubular bells—it always is the singer within me crying to get out.

What does the Pulitzer mean? It means the kind of honor which allows your basic fee to go up. Beyond that, it's a joy to play with, like a new sled, which you finally put away and go back to work.

You're a most prolific worker, aren't you? In spurts. I will have had seven major premieres in twelve months, but that windfall is mainly due to the Bicentennial frenzy which already is subsiding. The seven works, though of different sonic species, are thematically related inasmuch as they all spouted from one flow. The first, a grand symphonic affair called *Assembly and Fall*, was played last autumn by the magnificent North Carolina Orchestra. Then came *Air Music*. *Book of Hours*, for flute and harp, had its first performance in February. One week later in Kennedy Center the coruscating Emanuel Ax premiered my *Eight Piano Etudes*. *Serenade* for voice, viola, violin and piano, commissioned by a group in Akron, was first heard there last month, and this month *Sky Music* for solo harp gets launched in Albuquerque. The seventh and last new work, and the closest to my heart, is a large set of songs called *Women's Voices*, which Joyce Mathis will sing here next November. It is, so to speak, an uncomfortable privilege—a pleasurable torture—to sit in the audience and hear a really good performer execute one's intimate sounds, hitherto so private, now hopelessly public.

Your brash, outspoken Diaries *are a public part of your-self too, yet you have vetoed discussion of your personal life in this interview. Why?* My literary outspokenness, if such it be, is a mode of art which cannot extend to published conversation. I'm a very closed person, really, and surely your *Times* readers are above prurience. Besides, the *Diaries* belong to the past, as does that form of brashness which is youth's prerogative. Meanwhile I do have four printed books of objective essays which no one reads, but which are also a part of myself.

You say there is no more Establishment. Where do you fit into the spectrum of your musical peers? You'd have to ask the peers. Or rather, objective bystanders. Some of those so-called peers have no use for me, although I admire them, while others seem perversely overrated. One can't know what people say behind one's back, but by and large composers' opinions about each other's work are no longer voiced *ex cathedra* from rival camps. Rather than belittle each other's dialects, they concentrate on how the dialects are phrased. There are exceptions. If a Boulez, for instance, does not take seriously a certain sort of tonal melodism, I myself am in-capable of digging electronics or aleatorics. Anyway, I've never run with the pack, composing according to fashion; I've always been a lone wolf, composing according to need. The Red Queen said you've got to run fast to stay in one place. I stayed in one place. Now it's clear I've run fast.

What one American composer do you most love? Paul Bowles.

What American singers do you admire? How tell the singer from the song? Insofar as we applaud music rather than the glittering bodies from which music issues, I admire Phyllis Curtin because she knows how to utter English, a rarer gift than you might suppose. Let me quickly add Beverly Wolff, Betty Allen, Susan Davenney, Elaine Bonazzi, Bethany Beardslee, Cathy Berberian, Judith Raskin, Jan de Gaetani, Phyllis Bryn-Julson. Fewer known male singers are so special, though Donald Gramm and Charles Bressler come to mind. As for superstars, Leontyne Price is unique in giving even a remote damn about today's music. Indeed, Price is the only American opera diva who has any notion of song, thanks partly to her training as an intelligence rather than as a computerized triller. As representatives of vital music, there are no superstar mezzos in our country. One British Janet Baker equals a dozen Marilyn Hornes. It might be useful to note here that my lifelong affair with songwriting stems from a love not of singing but of poetry. Virtuosity for its own sake accounts for my indifference to *bel canto* literature, and perhaps for my failure thus far to create a viable opera in the soap tradition. I'm incapable of musicalizing words whose literary value I don't believe in. The texts of most arias embarrass me no less than the expository parts of librettos.

How about music critics? There are fewer decent critics than decent composers in the U.S. today. Using Virgil Thomson as an absolute, only three or four critics come up to par. They share Thomson's perception, and may even exceed his scope, but none boasts his unquenchable panache —his gift for cracking square center with that perfect little Fabergé hammer. No good critic is now, as Virgil was (and remains), also a composer activated from within the core of sound, endowing his subject with compassion rather than with contempt, or, at the very best, with musicological cant. A critic's chief crime, as composers see it, rests in a casual viewpoint toward new music. Admittedly most new music, like most everything, is mediocre and the critic must say so; but let him say so with sorrow, not sarcasm. His problem is partly occupational, for good criticism abounds in related fields. Movie, art, dance and drama critics review mostly the new. Only music critics must still think up phrases for Beethoven because only they review performance equally with what's performed. In other arts the past is exception; in music the past is rule. Music reviewing is music rehearing.

Dare I ask where you think music is heading? Behind that familiar question lurks a modern uneasiness, as though art had a moral obligation to endure (a conclusion which would never have occurred to Bach), while suspecting that only a fraction of it deserves room in a time capsule. There also lurks a modern implication that art, as a value, is precarious —that it should last but won't. Well, a mere composer is the last person to question, since, by definition, he's in no position to see beyond his nose. That answer is evasive, for I flatter myself that I'm more than a mere composer. However, the matter doesn't concern me much. Replies to such questions invariably prove fallacious within a year. Still, trends are clear. For example, scandal in music seems to be gone. Earlier in the century the biggest *causes célèbres* were scandals, and all except *Sacre* were vocal works: *Pierrot, Noces, Wozzeck, Four Saints.* But those sixties firecrackers of, say, Berio and Salzman and Austin spluttered insofar as they offered themselves as outrageous. Perhaps the scandal of Vietnam dwarfed such adventures. In any case true scandal can't be planned, and might come today only via the quintessentially pristine. Meanwhile the current example of an *enfant terrible* is not even an Alice Cooper or a loud Lukas Foss, but a muffled Morton Feldman or a gentle George Crumb.

Are you pleased with yourself? My self-assured tone clothes an insecurity. I know my worth, yet that worth lies in past works which now lead their own life and no longer concern me. I feel unprotected and, in spite of dear friends, alone. I no longer smoke, drink, carouse or go to parties. Sugar is my sole vice and reading my joy. My mind is on work, or related elements, twenty-four hours a day, which accounts for the egocentricity of all artists and hides them from their own vulnerability. No, I'm not pleased with myself, because I'm continually alarmed by the ongoing present of which I am a part.

Does politics enter into art? How does it not? Musicians can be as dumb as anyone, but they are surely no dumber, and as a rule have quicker instincts than "real" people. But as for Big Statements, artists shouldn't bother, since they all, no matter how sterile or derivative, reflect the times simply by dint of inhabiting the times.

What are you working on now? Orchestration of a mini-opera for the National Endowment. The scenario by Jim Holmes is based on Kenneth Koch's *Hearing*, which I set to music years ago. I also have three books in the oven: another diary, a batch of essays about esthetics, and a treatise on song. This summer I'd like to do a long organ piece and think about a new opera. I will never *never* NEVER write another soap opera of sound effects smeared on a European classic like *Miss Julie* (though that's all opera companies take chances on), but I might consider some Forster novel. After that, I have no ideas. Have you any?

My dear Ned Rorem, who are you? My dear John Gruen, who is anyone? The search for an answer keeps us forever evolving—which accounts for the poignance of Madame Du Barry's last words, "Just one more moment, Mister Headsman." I don't know who I am, but I've a notion of what I am. The what is a special fact, distorted through one's personal lens, then flashed, for better or worse, into the world.

4·Criticism

People resent my diary for not divulging conversations with those whose names I "merely" drop. Yet there's nothing to divulge. Artists of stature together talk money and health and sex, occasionally politics if they're petitioning funds for Israel or against Vietnam, but never, never esthetics. Esthetics is the priority of beginners and has no place in the bull sessions of professionals—only in their work. As for the diary not containing what it means to be an artist: that meaning presumably is in my music. The reviewer need not be blamed for ignoring my sixty-odd published essays and four published collections on non-diary matters. But then, what qualifies him as a reviewer?

When *The Paris Diary* came out, Harold Acton, who loathed it, asked: "...what have such horrors as crabs, piles, and bedbugs to do with musical inspiration and 'the crushing necessity to be an artist'?" How should I know? I'm the artist, he's the esthete.

The most quoted phrase of my least quoted book, *Pure Contraption:* "Critics of words use words. Critics of music use words."

Critics of critics use words. John Simon phoned this evening to say he was enjoying WNCN's Birthday Salute to me. In the background, behind the phone's static and John's Transylvanian syllables, I did detect the ripple of my *Barcarolles.* Should one tell a composer *during* his music that one likes the music? John does believe in hissing plays, but only *after* a performance.

Plays and music are to be booed at or clapped for. Can you applaud a painting?

No one imagines himself to be without humor. To claim that you lack humor is already a humorous notion—humor being an ability to see three sides of one coin, a coin shaped like a tear.

But in music nothing is more elusive than humor. Judging from last night's "opera," *The W. of Babylon,* Wuorinen too is on the wrong path—a path all the more uncomfortable in being paved with coy intentions. (Stanley Silverman aims lower but hits the same target dead center.) Even were his Firbankian libretto livelier, Wuorinen's craggy language would be at odds with it. Just as twelve-tone music —though vast in tragic potential—can never be funny, neither can consistently ugly music depict whimsy. (Mozart is ugly only part of the time.) I used to feel I missed the might of Wuorinen's art—it was my lack. But there *is* no might, it's bluff. Or is it still my lack? Like Kosinski he's skilled in the wiles of PR men. His clique, each dead-serious hairy member of which resembles him to a T, breaks up on cue like a TV laugh track. Of course it's unfair (voluptuously unfair) to judge a man by a single flop, especially if he's had successes. Yet one errant brick can destabilize a monument, and I have loathed upstanding citizens for the sounds they make when swallowing water. Just as John Simon poisons a well-reasoned essay by a jibe at an actress, so, I imagine, do my diaries—or some mere paragraphs therein (perhaps this very sentence)—disqualify a life's work in music.

Can the One Rotten Apple theory apply to the test of esthetics? Can one unfocused moment in the otherwise unblurred intuition of a respected person contaminate the respect, especially if the focus is professionally aimed? Can Simon's championing of Lina Wertmuller put into doubt his whole work? Can Andrew Porter's nearsighted view of Crumb today raise questions about his farsightedness yesterday? Sadly, one false step can, for a critic, demean his whole *oeuvre*, even as Hugues Cuénod's vocal artistry is diminished by his continually singing with inept accompanists. And what about creative artists? Ravel, the canniest jeweler of our century, never allowed his duds to greet the public; but the posthumous printing of his early forays now casts a gray light—at least for me—upon the perfection of his later masterpieces. Perhaps it's unfair to disillusion the public with professional secrets (those last-minute formal hints by "noncreative" advisers which made whole pieces jell), although most of us, artists and otherwise, are judged by flops and not by triumphs.

I judge all art the same way first: by whether I believe it. If I believe it I'll nudge further to see if I believe *in* it. Honesty of tone preempts honesty of content.

Wertmuller. Not for a second do I believe she believes

what she purports to "say" so much as she believes in the veneer of Love Me, Italian style. Now, because I feel she doesn't believe herself, I don't believe her either, so obviously I don't believe *in* her.

John Simon, in his (justifiable) treatise on the esthetics of the actor's appearance, states: "A homely actress is always driven to *act* beautiful, and this is precisely what no beautiful woman ever does." (By beautiful woman one assumes he means beautiful actress. Nor does he anywhere pose the problem of a beautiful actress portraying a homely woman.) Yes, but a beautiful actress must *act* beautiful too—in a manner different from, even opposed to, her own "kind" of beauty. (Could Margaret Leighton have portrayed Marilyn Monroe?) Beauty's not endowed with built-in confidence, strange as this seems to the plain. Only stupidity provides confidence. Smart beauties are socially uneasy. Despite Simon's feelings to the contrary (and he admits bias toward women; nowhere is there question of men), it's irrefutable that "plain" women can give convincing illusions of beauty, certainly in opera. What Simon bemoans is probably not lack of beauty but lack of class.

"Is nothing sacred?" asks a letter to the *Times* chastising Simon for chastising Ruth Gordon. No, nothing is sacred. What takes Ruth Gordon beyond criticism, at sixteen bucks a ticket?

Lunch with Gore Vidal (in America to plug his new book and—who knows?—to run as a White House candidate). I tell him with what dismay one reads the recent high-culture interviews with the paltry Wertmuller. "Yes, isn't she paltry," agrees Gore. "Last week in Rome I was at Rossellini's when Wertmuller, just back from New York, telephoned.

Rossellini said, 'Lina, *Il Messaggero* tells us that some woman in America who says she's Lina Wertmuller has been advertising herself as the world's greatest movie director. Look into this, it's bad business.' "

Early this morning on emerging from the County Court House where against my desire I had enrolled for jury duty, I bought *New York* magazine with the faint hope of finding a review, however brief and bad, of my two birthday concerts. In the taxi I read a sizable critique—the sort for which your most indulgent fantasies yearn vainly. Unqualifiedly Alan Rich takes my defense, absolves me, so to speak, from the crime of being me, and by so doing, he not only justifies my "American worth" to critical foes who confound persona with product but admits to a covert longing to *be* me (as I want to be Doris Day). Reaction? Disbelief, embarrassment, thrill. How could I dream that the up-to-date Alan might allow that grammar, rather than language, contains what is intrinsically vicious or virtuous in music, and that I am mostly a grammarian? Still, no one's as virtuous as he claims me to be. I've always found his journalistic horniness enticing, and here he commits himself now in the eyes of the world to one who might not live up to such standards. Like being raped (happily) in the County Court House, this second-best review of my adulthood.

Good reviews don't make me feel as good as bad ones make me feel bad. Writing up poems is to write poems. Reviewing concerts is writing down. (Occasionally a Tovey rises high, but not as a reviewer.) What is one to think of, learn from, the contradictions in various professional criticisms of the same music? Allen Hughes talks of me warmly, Henahan icily. Where Schonberg is pecksniffian, Rich is magnanimous. The *Post* reviews most everything I compose, the *Voice* nothing, ever. Being a sometime critic, I know the breed's human. The difference between specimens of the breed is that some write well, some don't. Few speak for hearer.

Three features distinguish the music reviewer from reviewers of other arts. He deals with the ephemeral. He hears mostly works of the past. He is often a practitioner, as well as critic, of his art.

Nearly every concert is a one-shot deal: it will not be repeated here tomorrow for another public, or next week, or ever. An art show lasts long enough for maximum attendance. A new ballet remains in repertory till season's end. So it is, too, with movies and (theoretically) plays. But with music the surefirest hit gets heard only once, even with famous soloists. A Gielgud alone on stage reciting Shakespeare fills the hall for weeks, but could a Horowitz have a run with one Beethoven program night after night in Carnegie? The question doesn't arise; it's not in the nature of the game. The music critic therefore, unlike theater or painting critics, is not a foretaster. He writes epitaphs rather than birth notices.

The contemporary audience of Handel was not concerned with Machaut. Schubert's fans were not concerned with Handel. But today's Music Lovers place past composers above and before present composers. Right or wrong, this is endemic. Bach may thus be correctly termed a twentieth-century musician. I don't mean this metaphorically—that he answers to our needs. We hear him as he never heard himself; we perform him in the now, with mannerisms of now. Our Bach is actually closer to Berio than to the Bach of 1785, and is absorbed with intervening wisdoms and delusions. I knew Billie Holiday before I knew Bach so I still hear him conditioned by the fact of her—his bluesy chords, those wailing tunes.

Familles, je vous hais, said Gide. Music Lovers, I loathe you.

I've never trained myself to listen critically with the intention of forming verbal ideas about music. I hear kinetically rather than intelligently, or else I don't listen at all. (I *have*—though none too happily—trained my ears to turn off.) Response to what I hear is as much reaction as opinion. Trained reaction, not dreams. For a composer, as distinct from reviewer or executant or mere Music Lover, such reaction tends toward what is played rather than how it's played.

It is not opinion but fact that Menotti single-handedly revitalized the concept of living opera for Americans. Thanks solely to the example of his success in the 1940s, dozens of operas appeared by other composers hoping to hit the jackpot. Two or three were even good. The effort persists after three decades and it is safe to state that Menotti, whatever the final worth of his own output, violently altered the nature of lyric theater here, and by extension of musical art throughout the world.

Throughout that same world his own operas are still played; from the standpoint of ratings he has no complaints. Yet to the *Times* he recently wailed long and loud about the endlessly derisive tone of his critical reception. Indeed, so discouraged is he with his adopted country that at sixty-three he plans to expatriate himself. However petulant the reason, his action is sad.

Critic Henahan meanwhile relieves himself on the situa-

tion. He does not say, "Come back, all is forgiven," nor
"Farewell and thanks," nor even "Good riddance." That
Menotti should presume to take himself seriously, Henahan
takes in turn as an affront, avenging himself through devious
witticisms.

"Why," wonders Menotti, "have there been twenty-five
years of uninterrupted triumphs of *The Consul* all over the
world?" Rather than give a straight answer (namely, that the
piece's theatricality defies erosion), Henahan begrudges
Menotti his due. "As if age and popularity sanctified," he
answers, then defrauds his own truism by declaring that
"*Abie's Irish Rose,* in its time, had a great many more performances than *The Consul,* and nowadays there is no
twenty-five-year-old movie so terrible that someone will not
bring it back. . . ." Don't we also bring back good movies?
Didn't certain pieces of Beethoven die far younger than *The
Consul?*

Composers are too sensitive to criticism, Henahan suggests, when "any small arrow . . . is magnified into something
as . . . deadly as Wotan's spear." Briefly he holds back his
own small arrow, then lets fly: ". . . the feebleness of [Menot-
ti's] music itself [is a matter] in which a wide diversity of
opinion would be surprising."

What wounds Henahan in return is Menotti's accusation
that critics forever repeat "the same old boring clichés."
This he allows, quickly bringing up Rubinstein as someone
for whom "the same old boring clichés want to tumble out,"
justified by the elegant image that "repetition is the gravy
on which art floats." But if Rubinstein literally repeats his
programs, Menotti does so only metaphorically. A composer,
from year to year, does try to come up with something a bit
more varied than do standard virtuosos, who are never
castigated for lack of adventure. He may not speak a new

language each time, but at least he tries for—let's call them —fresh clichés.

Henahan presumes to liken himself to Homer, then inquires, "Who denigrates Wagner for dragging in the Rhinegold motif several thousand times during the *Ring?*" As though the motif Wagner "drags" in were a mere repetition, a mere unchanged bromide irrelevant to the organic evolution of a given work of art (for Wagner does not use this motif in, say, *Tristan* or *Meistersinger*). Recovering himself, Henahan then asks, "Who condemns a mouse for always emitting the same squeak?" Does a mouse? And if "even the greatest composers mimic themselves endlessly," why punish Menotti? And why vouchsafe an argument by hiding behind Ernest Newman's remark that a composer will "unconsciously fall back on a formula" (which is, of course, true), when formula does not mean motif, much less cliché.

A critic's duty is to inform the world at large about the integrity of the world of art as he comprehends this through his own integrity. If a new piece of music is awful—and it usually is—a critic should react not with triumph but with tears. Henahan seemingly imagines that composers and critics are at war. His rules forbid that he salve those he wounds with constructive balm. He chalks up points in an imagined feud ("Menotti does not have to like the clichés of music critics; they do not have to like the clichés of *The Consul.* What, to coin a phrase, could be fairer?"), as indeed he imagines that composers feud among themselves (*viz* his recent remarks that the avant-garde will surely frown on Bernstein's *Dybbuk*—as though the avant-garde even existed any more to hand out demerits). Henahan is apparently the last to learn that years have passed since the various "schools" of composition sneered at each other on grounds of ideology. Composers today, whatever their persuasions, are magnanimous together, not contemptuous of each other's languages; they react only to how well the grammar —the cliché, if you will—of a given language is manipulated.

The *Times* may have been generous in allowing Menotti to voice his anxieties as a composer. Still we have lost him. Needless to say, it is a critic who has the last cliché.

There's Rembrandt's masterpiece. There it factually is, on the wall for all to admire or hate, interpret or misinterpret, and when the caretaker turns off the light and goes to sleep, there it still stays. But where—or rather, when—is Bach's masterpiece? On the page or in the resonant hall? Can Bach's or Rembrandt's masterpieces exist *as masterpieces* in memory, sight unseen, sound unheard? Can they exist as such to one who does not care for, or admit to, masterpieces? Can a masterpiece, like the caretaker's lamp, be turned off?

Will time tell? Is tenacity—as even the canniest critics conclude the frequent argument—the ultimate criterion for greatness? Will lesser critics be buried beneath the trash they've praised?

Well, Gide (who gambled wrong on Proust) once declared that if, like all French youth, he hadn't been weaned on the "greatness" of Rimbaud, it's not sure that—come upon cold—the greatness would have struck him *d'emblée*. Gide did laud many a forgotten mediocrity, as did many another first-rate artist before and after him.

Is Shakespeare great because he's lasted? What about Marlowe, who's lasted too, but is forty times less read? Is Marlowe a fortieth less great? Is Dryden half as great? If Bach is great because he's lasted, was he, in the abstract, as great during his eighteenth-century period of eclipse? Buxtehude lasted just as long, and Machaut twice as long. Is

Machaut's longevity a sign of greatness, or a sign of usable history?

Could Plato's music, if we had it, have been greater than Bach's? By its nature sculpture is the most durable art; is sculpture therefore the greatest art?

That word greatness is a fly in the ointment. The argument's one of fluid esthetics, not of concrete absolutes. Different ages, different needs. I, for one, have found that even my taste, which I thought invincible, has shifted since childhood, finally. Those great movies are junk today, those Haydn quartets a long, long bore. Trash, meanwhile, can be mighty durable, and time, as Auden pointed out, will say nothing but I told you so.

As for the canniest of critics, are they, as they claim, more qualified than us mortals? Can long experience, can forty viewings of forty Hamlets render a critic more sensitive than our lone viewing renders us? Lautréamont literally had not the time to mellow, and mellowness edges quick into rot.

The inspired Susan Sontag contends that "The pathos that all works of art reek of comes from their historicity . . . from our awareness that no one would or could ever do *that* again." Including, one might add, the artist. Looking at his own work of thirty years ago, or even of yesterday, he sadly notes that although he could never repeat certain infantile errors, neither could he retrieve certain strokes of luck in just those ways. (Some are tempted to err in the present by revising the past. Paul Goodman's late editing of his youthful poems is a crime of misjudgment: with one mere change of word in, say, *The Lordly Hudson,* he literally wrenches the poem from us and back to himself.) But doesn't the pathos of anything—bad art as well as good, a love affair, a dead friend, a long-ago meal, youth itself—

come from historicity? Are works of art the more pathetic for having "survived"? And have they indeed survived with any patina of their initial purpose?

Pictures, like music, are made to be referred to again (although pictures, unlike music, can be referred to more easily through memory alone: enlarge that snapshot on the brain a fraction of a second, but music needs the time it needs). A person who hears and rehears *Tosca* thrice or forty times, a Poulenc song a hundred times in forty new renditions, is normal, normal, and pictures hang on our walls all day and night. But a person who returns once or twice— let alone forty times—to a movie is some kind of a nut. Yet aren't movies healthier? Etc.

Before falling to sleep (from which I was, at 2:30, to wake up screaming from that too-keen-for-comment nightmare) I savored the skilled intensity of Pauline Kael in her diatribe against the "moguls." She does skirt one point: that people get (as they got Nixon) what they deserve. And though she allows that better movies are being born now in America than at any time anywhere, and reaffirms the obvious that hits are not to be confused with art, she avoids admitting that the vast movie public never was, nor can be, by definition, discriminating. (The young, she claims, have had their taste waylaid in the past two years; but have they ever really been *nuancé* as she gives them credit? On summer beaches now as from winter porches then, show us one, just one, of those thousand lovely children attending to the Debussy Trio as to the rock background. *Le Sacre* could fill their every visceral requirement, but where is it?) Otherwise, of course, she's right about moguls slapping poets for being poets. In music the moguls (i.e., performers' impresarios) are unaware of the very existence of poets (i.e., composers), and the word artist has come to mean entertainer.

To be a movie critic is to investigate, like a telescope, the inherently expanding, because film, no matter how "fine," is through its size construed for *le grand public*—the collective eye. To be a music critic is to examine, like a microscope, the infinitely small (and how many contracting universes float on that lens!), because a piece, no matter how gross, is construed for the unique ear. Only when music relinquishes its function as an aural art (something to be attended) and caters to the whole body (an accompaniment) does it cease being a fine art.

No one has written, but somebody should, an esthetic history of movie music. Seeing *Of Human Bondage* again (what marshmallows we swallowed once from the lips of Leslie Howard, yet what techniques had Bette Davis even then!), all to the afflicting notes of Max Steiner, you realize how inappropriate such music has become. Music makes or breaks the weakest, the strongest, film. The sixties' taste of the European masters: Antonioni used only factory whistles or "source" tunes from radios; Fellini, only Rota's witty scores for even his saddest tales; Bergman (with his sense of the apropos in *Cries and Whispers*), only Chopin and Bach. Bertolucci, with the languorous Delerue, confirms that the most avant-garde use the most arrière-garde music. (Satie. Cocteau's taste. Use of jazz in the fifties' tragedies. Why they worked, why they didn't. Etc. Endlessly complex as a study on the employment of form and color in the Renaissance.)

Deep in the dust I retrieved that vanished *New Directions* of 1936 devoted to surrealism and including Olga Rudge's rough translation of Jean Cocteau's slick *Laic Mystery*.

France detests the supernatural [claimed Jean]. Mr. Maskelin, director of the Mystery Theater of London ... placed a pane of glass on the backs of two chairs, on this he builds a little cupboard sixty centimeters high and one more meter wide showing us the boards back and front. The cupboard is open at the top. He shuts a bell inside and orders it to ring. The bell rings. Then an invisible hand shakes the bell out of an aperture on top. This same invisible hand seizes a basque drum, and throws out a handkerchief after having knotted it three times. The Empire public laughed and hissed ... "there is someone inside." But the turn doesn't hinge on the fact that there is no one inside, but on the fact that someone is between the boards where his presence is inexplicable because of their size and position. "There is someone there, there is someone there, take it off." This cruel and stupid public was incapable of bringing its mind to bear on the point that made the turn an enigma.

Even when wrong Cocteau is right. Yet he's not right here. He could have translated the public's reaction as gullible rage. To believe someone's in the cupboard is to believe the unbelievable, and that is not stupid but fanciful. Similarly the American public thrills like infants when the lights, one by one, begin to glimmer in the dollhouse of *Tiny Alice*.

Harold Clurman, in quoting Cocteau, who cites a Chinese proverb, "Genius creates hospitals," takes this to mean: A host of lesser men becomes warped in imitation of the greater one. Too many instances of genius feeding off the originality of lesser men disprove this interpretation. Where would the "inventions" of Wagner or Debussy be without those of a Spohr or a Rebikov? It's because lesser men, who possess only novelty, become blind with despair at the dazzling uses to which a great man puts their novelty that hospitals are built.

It seems unfair to judge by first reactions, yet for me, in matters of art, those reactions seldom alter with time. Occasionally I'll come round, as for Brahms and Beckett. Though whenever I stab anew at, say, Faulkner or Berlioz, I'm baffled, not at what they are in themselves, but at what other people—delicately wise people—find in them.

Last night masochism urged me to reconsider *Le Partage de Midi*. Claudel too remains what he always seemed: a sophomoric *composeur* with no sense of shape. The lavishness of his banality, the sexist simplicity of his Catholic heart, pushed to such limits turn triteness to fright. That he allowed no abridgments of those redundant ohs and ahs, that he lived to such a ripe age, is due to the fact that he "got out of himself" by sitting through his endless plays (only economists die young), while the audience feared for its own vanishing youth.

Unlike inspired cuisine from mediocre staples, a good production cannot hide faults of a "literary" play; it can only heighten them. But wow! that marvelous *mise en scène* at the Comédie Française. Was it 1954? There, like yesterday, stands Edwige Feuillère, whose slightest pattern moved mountains, and there is Félix Labisse's set. Was ever decor more apt? Balthus' maybe, for *L'Île des chèvres*, or Noguchi's for the Graham dance about Saint Joan? Or Bill Ritman's for the second scene of *Tiny Alice?*

Since for years I've derided Hemingway, to refresh my mind for future derision I just reread a dozen of his stories, and liked them. Suddenly they're in context, classic, assessable. He wasn't a poet, nor even somehow a novelist, but a playwright who didn't write plays. His unmistakable gift was a good ear—that is, an absence of imagination.

Advance reviews of the new book are more snide than for previous books. "The self he exhibits," declares the Kirkus Service, "belongs to a world of artifice, finds Rochas cologne truer than roses, and seems to require the diaries for completion." Fair enough. I prefer perfume to plants just as I prefer Frescobaldi to folksong, for I am not drawn to raw material but to what can be made from it. More disconcerting is to be taken literally, to have each phrase witlessly deciphered as though I had *meant* the phrase. "For how much longer can he entice the boys with his black T-shirt?" the review asks (the boys, indeed! as though that slur were still in coinage), and goes on to warn: "An involvement for consenting adults."

But if there's a grain of truth in every lie, there's a bushel in any opinion, no matter how stupid. Perhaps simply the book does not give off the tone intended. With all the contrivance the tears are real. But if I cannot bear for my sarcasms to be taken sarcastically, neither can I with any potency defend my diary within my diary.

Spender's serialized *Notebook* in *London Magazine* holds the attention, yet makes me dimly uneasy with its unflagging highmindedness. Is this because I feel that as he plows through life Spender does have fancies beyond (or beside) those of grand art and the need to be useful, or because my own notebooks seem so *déclassés*—so unnecessary—by comparison?

In his current reflections on Venice, for instance, he observes what I never observe, finds continual connections between then and now, both personal and general, and has the discipline of history as voucher for opinions. Still it's a poet talking, and though one can't begrudge his urge for immortal utterance (since it takes one to know one, I spot his diarist's tricks in a trice—avoidance of dropping names by arranging to have his own name dropped, here by Peggy Guggenheim, or there by total strangers in Harry's Bar), he's sometimes prosaically wrong. He hears like an author just as I see like a musician, but he makes the layman's fatal error of comparing the arts. For example, in an interestingly careless paragraph about Venetian painters he contends that "Both allegorists and symbolists use visual imagery or symbolism as poets often use them. . . . When Shelley saw eyes instead of nipples in his wife's breasts, he was merely projecting upon the external world the way in which images were juxtaposed in his poetry. A picture of breasts with nipples as eyes would seem surrealist, but not a line in poetry such as 'Thy paps are like eyes in thy breasts.' This use of associations springing from the unconscious is conventionally poetic. It is only when it is applied to painting that it seems surrealist. . . ." Let's overlook that what Spender says of Shelley ("saw eyes instead of nipples") and what Shelley actually said ("Thy paps are like eyes") is to confuse metaphor with simile. What Spender forgets is that language is itself symbolic, painting is not, which is why painting, like music, is not "translated." The word "bird" symbolizes (is a metaphor for) a bird. The painting of a bird signifies (is a representation of) a bird—or *uccello, oiseau, pájaro,* Vogel, and to a Chinese or Pole is a bird, whatever they name it. And however "abstracted," a bird is a bird is a vogel. For painting is never metaphor. Since language is always metaphor, literary surrealism is always less startling than to the eye. And music? Is music symbolic? Symbolic of what? (JH says I'm too fussy about all this. That anyway a painting has never made him cry, while books and music have.)

I cannot not refrain from consulting an old agenda to confirm that on that snowy noon of February third in 1951 I took Julius Katchen to lunch at Stephen's in Saint John's Wood, and Natasha Litvin for dessert played us Barber's new sonata, and we were all warm toward each other. Then the Spenders at three o'clock came with us to Wigmore Hall, where Julius played the London premiere of my new sonata, after which, and during the ensuing quarter-century, Stephen's been cool toward me.

What is it that makes so-called experimental prose more unviable than experimental music or pictures? The fact that language, already imprecise and metaphoric, cannot lend itself to distortion the way notes and images can? Notes and images mean themselves. Language symbolizes something beyond itself. The appearance of versified poetry (though not necessarily its sound or its sense) can seem dumb—dumber, certainly, than abstract pictures.

The art of the written word, even of the spoken language, is less susceptible to fooling around than other arts are. Print (speech) is already a *representation*, which no other art is (music's final state, unlike literature's, is not in the printed score but in the execution of the printed score), so we don't need symbols of symbols. Because of this symbolism every reader visualizes (symbolizes) his own scenes: the same words evoke different pictures for every reader. With movies and paintings and music one viewer or listener may react and interpret differently from another viewer or listener, but what he sees or hears is identical to what another sees or hears.

In Pittsburgh last week Donald Johanos conducted *Air Music*. Apone's review stunned me. "The Pittsburgh Symphony," he writes, "keeps promoting Rorem's music even though his orchestral efforts have never deserved the continued performance he gets here.... In view of Rorem's showings here over the years, it would seem time to say enough." Five years ago, when my Piano Concerto was premiered, he wrote: "... one of the finest new works heard here in years.... One of those intense, intelligent, dashing, bracing works which is wonderfully aglow." *Air Music* he terms "indistinguishable from noise [by a] cynical trickster [and] audience despiser," while the Concerto showed "superior craftsmanship stamped on every bar as the restless energy runs the six movements." What can a composer learn from this? JH nicely feels that "the critics" don't hear what in fact my music declares. If more stylish composers are heeded according to verbal terms specifically stated by themselves, and thus of necessity reacted to with new and trained ears, my music, because I state no terms, is listened to "in the old way." Yet in fact (adds JH) the signature of my music is that it never builds ahead to climax, but *is*, continually is, in all its density, and thus cannot be heard the old way. Well, that makes sense, but I didn't say it. Withdraw and alienate friends. Perhaps Apone hates me for moral reasons, the sins of prose strangle me, but no, I cannot not.

I despise Anaïs Nin for the best of reasons: her diaries sell and mine don't. I'll not begrudge a glory earned: If Nin were more than the Ann Landers of words, more than the bated breath of humorless debs, I might applaud. My contempt is for high place ill-gained, while realizing this to be more the "fault" of a gullible public—or of press agentry— than of the artist's ambition. Success to me means not value but function in relation to packaging. Nin sells, that's her purpose. The fact that James Joyce, finally, sells too, does not make him a success, since literature's purpose is not glorious or monetary, like rock music's. (*Anteus* magazine is a success, since its purpose—to circulate among two thousand readers—has been fulfilled.)

From *Das Wohltemperierte Klavier*, which daily after decades I admire unqualifiedly, the Preludes bring more pleasure than the Fugues. Is this because all fugues, no matter by whom, become, after their initial statements, rather predictable, being propelled less by inspirational sweep than by device? For fugue is device, not form. And even fugues by Bach—for whom the device was more a need than for, say, Reger—on patterns dictated by angels can only go here or there, not just anywhere, while his preludes lead thrillingly where angels fear to tread.

Christmas party at Boosey & Hawkes. Quaintance Eaton, eyes the same hue as her evergreen crown, which in turn echoes the jade ropes at her throat, approaches—having read an advance copy of my review of *Bagázh*—and, agreeably holding me in her green gaze, declares: "I liked your phrase that great artists save their greatness for their art and don't squander it in conversation, even with each other. But how do you account for your own conversation?" Answers: a) Nothing is squandered, since you are not aware of what is *withheld* from the conversation; b) My greatness *is* the conversation; c) Who says my art's great?; d) Who says my conversation's great?

In Charles Rosen's book on Schoenberg he allows as to how the primary means of expressivity is dissonance, and agrees that twelve-tone music doesn't, in the classical sense, contain dissonance since it doesn't contain the consonance against which dissonance is defined; yet he contends that Schoenberg's music is vastly expressive because Schoenberg willfully imposed, through his superior melodies . . . etc. In fact, melodies of Debussy, Ravel, Britten, Poulenc, Messiaen, are all post-Pfitzner, and superior to Schoenberg's melodies, at least by my standard, which is no less sensitive than Rosen's. He's having it both ways. Either Schoenberg's melodies are expressive in some new way not expressed or they're inexpressive. But Rosen suggests they're expressive in the old way—through consonance as relief from dissonance.

If you were wondering why suddenly last Sunday Harold Schonberg's sermon gave off a sheen of quality, it is because, without my permission and without my name, he quoted intact a personal letter from me to him. The letter, not cranky but curious, examined the subject of Idea in Music, Schonberg having recently suggested that not only my music but that of other contemporaries "lacked ideas." Well, he may not admire my musical ideas, but when he pads his column with my literary ones I need to cry out. How? Even this paragraph sounds petulant. At least I've cut it down to one tenth its original length; and when I plagiarize I change wording, order of notes: that's all there is to art.

Suppose there weren't any more Ideas in our galaxy. Yet insofar as no two people are the same, any old ideas in new heads take on a separate—an original—gloss. As to whether the gloss is inspired, or even very diverting, is a moot question. But everything is always new under the sun.

How repugnant is the easy laugh. At P.E.N. last evening, "The Continuing Presence of Frank O'Hara," chaired by

Richard Howard and featuring Jane Freilicher, Larry Rivers, John Ashbery and Kenneth Koch all looking exquisitely their age, failed to catch fire. Frank's been dead ten years. Here was a public reminiscence, not a memorial, by old friends for young fans who can't too much feel—nor need they—the nostalgia skirting specific poems which themselves contain the nostalgia. Still, all that is healthy. But oh, the easy laugh, the all-too-willing need to giggle knowingly at references to, say, Frank's adoration of what Larry called his "male children." Liberal sexism! If, as was contended, all Frank's poems were sexual (whose aren't?), why not then, without giggling, speak of the sex in his verses about girls? about tangerines and Sibelius? and about joy and sadness of the very verb and noun?

Came home to read further in Spender's diary. Again the easy laugh. He may well lament the ornery ignorance of his Florida undergraduates, but when Spender notes that "The only modern poets they seem to have heard of are Bob Dylan and Rod McKuen (if I spell his name correctly) . . ." the parentheses, like a pair of tongs, distance Spender in our eyes from what he finds offensive. He does, in fact, spell McKuen's name correctly, and knows it, yet feigns the same indifference which is real in the students, and which he reproaches them for. How little we learn from the great unwashed, and how even less from our peers.

5. *Vocabulary*

The phone intrudes like the person from Porlock, derailing my train of thought. A tenor, organizing a program around gay themes by gay composers, wonders if I will contribute. Certainly not. I'm a composer, not a gay composer. Sexuality may relate to an artist's becoming an artist, but not to his becoming a good artist. I want to be loved or hated, not for my nature, but for the quality of my nature. Anyone can be gay—it's no accomplishment—but only I can be me. (A concert of straight composers might be a novelty.)

I am not We, and am unable to verbalize collectively, much less identify with even such groups as composers or lovers. I can't say "we composers" or "my lover and me," but "lovers are," "composers are," "Americans are," "they are." Do I dread not being unique? With gays, I think Them, not Us. How can They, inherently more diverse than a Zulu tribe or even than an international bourgeoisie, merely magnify, with We, a sole thread of their complex web? I resent vouchsafing individuality even to such a category as Mankind (still, what can you do?), but classify myself as a homo-sapient musician who is sexual. The sexual object is nobody's business, at least in public discussion. So diaries. If the goal of my drive becomes clear within their pages, such a "confession" is intended simply (simply?) as that of a human whose pangs of head and heart seem only too prevalent within the world's common groin.

Unlike negritude, homosexuality is not physically spottable, though gay clichés abound. A black when he's not Uncle Tomming is still black, and he's still black when he solves an algebraic equation. Is a queer queer when out of bed? When solving equations? Homosexuals have options: like heretics they can repent. A black cannot repent: he can only regret, or be proud.

Black Pride and Gay Pride are dangerous slogans, like White Pride or Straight Pride. Gay and black are not achievements but accidents of birth. One must not be ashamed, but that's not the same as being proud. Pride should lie only in what one does with one's blackness or gayness. Even so, has a straight or a white ever done anything to be proud of as a straight or a white?

Nor is the gay condition comparable to the female condition. A female remains so tomorrow. A lesbian (but who is not a lesbian?) may decide—consciously decide—not to be. Can change her mind. For a gay man to long to be treated like an unliberated woman is for him to have it both ways. A woman has no choice, but he can change his tune at any measure and never pay the piper.

How far must we discourage "isms" and promote tolerance? Is it antifeminist to be sexually unattracted to women?

Or blondist to dislike blonds? Must gerontophiles in fairness also covet kids? By extension embryos and corpses become fair game. Can we believe James Baldwin when he claims to have reached a utopian state when once, years ago, he was unaware that a friend of his was indeed Algerian until a test moment brought the fact home? Must humanity be so ideally One that we don't (aren't allowed to) distinguish sexually between mentalities, colors, ages, sexes, or even species? We smile when Gore Vidal, to the question "Was your first experience with a man or a woman?" answers "I thought it would be rude to ask." Do I, less young than last year, require gerontophiles? Could my fantasies not instead be for an ancient father embodied in that brawny young farmer there? But if in fact fantasies nourish us to that extent, what prevents the makeshift coition with virtually anything—jars of mercury, cobras, dynamite sticks?

Though turnabout may be fair play, men who like to "do anything" are as a rule of average intelligence, generous, congenial, but without much artistic force. Those whom in America we call "achievers" are as a rule carnally self-restricted, play one role, and have a knack for extended concentration on things not sexual. *L'homme moyen sensuel* is by definition less human than the "achiever," if by human we define the logic which differentiates man from other mammals. Sex has nothing to do with logic, but achievers treat sex logically (hence their roles) while average men treat sex sensually.

Just as there is no real literature recounting exploits from the viewpoint of the passive male (the *enculé*) so there is no real literature, beyond the blues of Ma Rainey, describing lesbian carnality. Has any woman related—with the necessity and anxiety and joy of a Goodman or a Ginsberg—the strictly physical charge of lesbianism? Can she? Can, in fact, the "passive" man make art from the trials of Eros? Yes. Since he exists he can be subject as well as object. Forster tried.

A man never knows quite who he is, but who he says he thinks he is gives a fair notion of who he thinks he is, if not, in fact, who he is.

In Susan Sontag's article "The Third World of Women," two points keep cropping up, as they always do among liberated women. The points are hardly minor, yet always incomplete:

1) Need for grammatical changes. Sontag composed the essay for translation into Spanish but didn't specify that the grammar she wrote about applied only to English. How would this read to Spaniards who know no English? That we say "he" when we mean either sex is meaningful only to someone who thinks in English. Admittedly this could stand change and would be comparatively easy to install among our habits, like using Ms. But although the woman's condition is an international condition, language conditions are not. The mind boggles at how to desexify a Latin tongue. If French doesn't have our pronoun problem, it does have gender for all nouns. Yet a French person born to the language doesn't *think* gender—that is, sex—as we, who have learned French as adults, do. Thus it doesn't strike a French person as funny that, say, most words both slang and medical for male organs are feminine (*la queue, la verge, la bitte,* etc.) while those for female parts are masculine (*le vagin, le con, le sein,* etc.). Diminutives, thought by Americans to be feminine, often turn masculine in French, i.e., *la mouche* becomes *le moucheron.* None of this is true for Italian,

which, however, has masculinized such eternally "female" things as the sea—*la mer*—which is *il mare*. That their nouns have gender (and that adjectives and certain verbs must agree) is not, French friends tell me, in any way sexual. As far as implication is concerned, one could substitute red noun or green noun for masculine noun and feminine noun. Agreeing then that gender quit the psychology of European languages long centuries back (just as it abandoned, along with the second person singular, our English language), how would other languages "treat" the feminist question?

2) For a woman to adopt her mother's family name as her own last name only means that she adopts her grandfather's name instead of her father's. Should you reply, Well, we've got to start somewhere, why not start with a brand-new name, as slaves did after the Civil War?

Why not eliminate Ms., along with Mrs. and Mr. and Master and Miss, and call everyone, as Quakers do, by both names?

French hardware stores sell signs saying *Chien Méchant* (Beware of Dog). As the case may be, should they not also sell a *Chienne Méchante*?

Asked by "outsiders" what word to use for the gay condition, what do I answer? Gay's not in my vocabulary, I wasn't raised that way. I've the right to say "queer" (but you have not), and "boy" and "girl," using them as the French do for every age. It's how you're brought up. (Chicago jargon used "jam" for "straight," "minty" for "dyke." Nor had I ever heard of garlic, limburger, pastrami, or pizza before moving to New York.) Must we alter vocabulary because the revolution tells us to? Paris may be worth a Mass, but who are those who dictate the Mass's dialect? All's in a name. Were our own names changed tomorrow we would wither.

Are women who act actors (or is that only men?), actresses (or is that for other species like tigress?), female actors (patronizing distinction?), or finally, yes, *faute de mieux*, actresses? We don't say authoress or Negress but we do say laundress and temptress. We don't say usheress or jeweleress but we do say duchess and seamstress. The French, of course, have the feminine of (most) every noun. But if they do have separate words, as we do, for bull and cow, they don't, as we do not, have the feminine for shark.

Sontag remarks, "I think now, looking back, that I don't really believe all the things I said in the essays I wrote in the 1960s." Where does that leave those whose consciousness was raised by her once novel concepts? Sontag was not, after all, a warm romancer, but a cool cataloguer (catalogueress?) of opinions (many, of course—like those on music—sounding as though she'd come to them yesterday) which she shouldn't belittle, if only for the sake of her converts. Or will the converts follow her bandwagon, not having learned from the early essays to think for themselves?

"The world loves drunks, but it despises perverts," Jane Bowles once sadly wrote. And indeed, alcoholics can always find companions, in crime if not in love. But I drank to find companions in love—or rather, to be found by them. Crucial distinction. Note the passive mode, *to be found* (which makes me feel sexy because guilty), a mode of Anglo-Saxon parlance but rare to the unguilty French. The unguilty French seldom refer to getting screwed or getting laid, that is, *être baisé*, but place that so-called passive act into the active mode: to get yourself laid, that is, *se faire baiser*. Anyway, strong-willed though I was (I command you to rape me!) I passed myself off as a vulnerable bit of lavender fluff longing to be—*comment dirai-je?*—to be, well, soiled.

The French have no word for straight, as counterpart (I almost wrote opposite) of gay. Nor have they an adjective like gay, preferring a noun or verb like *tante* or *en être*. And they have no words for crooked, shallow, vicarious, urge, or gentile. Crooked, as distinct from straight in its upright meaning, they must call *courbé* (curved), *sinueux*, or *tortueux*. Shallow becomes *peu profond*. Vicarious stems from our Protestant "vicar"—not a Catholic concern (they would say *vicieux*), which also is why gentiles are conveniently *chrétiens*. The closest thing to our verb "to urge" is their *exhorter*. From this paragraph draw no conclusions about the French; draw conclusions only about my conclusions about the French.

The French, however *vicieux*, are of all Europeans the most heterosexual.

Maldoror made love with a shark—a female shark, needless to say.

Women classically take their husband's name. Unmarried artists declare, "My work is my wife," and give their name to their creation. But the creation, no sooner spawned, goes off to live or die independently. Work is not spouse but offspring.

That paragraph reeks chauvinism. Artist implies male artist.

Does a female artist seek a mate? Could she conceivably think of her work as a husband? I, Ned Rorem, don't want a wife in any form (though at times I want a husband), and less and less do I want children—the desire to see my flesh

on other bones. My music's not my wife, nor my husband,
nor my child. My music is my music. Once composed it is
no longer even mine.

You open the *Times* and there, yet again, is the saga of
a sex transplant. There, yet again and sober as you please
in this bourgeois periodical, you see the photo of A New
Woman, muscular calves garnished with ankle hose, spit
curl embellishing a receding forehead, and rhetoric pro-
claiming that now at forty-five she is finally fulfilled—thanks
to hormones, penile mutilation, and an official receipt from
the Government. So you think, Well, poor dear, she must
be getting on: no one twenty today seems concerned with
sexual differences. Goodbye past, goodbye stardom, goodbye
O melting passive heroines enfolded by sculptured biceps
of the active heroes. What butch male will now defile this
fulfilled middle-aged female?

Then you fantasize a bit (though not for long) on possibilities. Suppose a man and woman are deeply in love.
Their only "obstacle" is that both are homophilic. Thus, the
carnal gratification—the final signature—is by nature denied
them. They separate. Now, such is the strength of absence
that each one reaches the same sacrificial conclusion. "If
she can only sexually be excited by women," says he to himself, "I'll become a woman." "If he can only be stimulated
by men," says she, "a man I shall be." But they ignore each
other's procedures. When next they meet he is (genitally)
a woman, she a man. Are they still in love? Where do they
go from here? Are they heterosexual? Who's on top?

You do grow weary of "courageous" announcements of
Homosexual Studies—of scientists achieving breakthroughs
on this "complex condition." Do the scientists have courses

in Heterosexual Studies? Might they then conclude that homosexuality is in fact a simple condition? That problem solved, they could go on to something important, like a cure for asthma.

As for the daring chic of the "new" bisexuality, why not talk of sexuality *tout court?* How about autosexuality for the Paul Newmans of this world? The term is more reasonable than the masturbatory *narcissism* for one who enjoys turning on all the sexes; such a person is not *attracted to,* such a person is *attracted to being attractive,* works well at it, and deserves all that she-he can get. (Not the love of self, but the love of being loved.)

It's been over forty years since in her witty verses on homosexuality Kay Boyle declared it "As engrossing as bee-raising/And as monotônous to the outsider." Like Alcoholics Anonymous, which is swell for stock-market analysts but not for poets, gay libbers are (rightly) more concerned with effects than causes. I couldn't stick A.A. because, being obsessed with the pound of cure, they never asked Why.

Isn't the "homosexual condition" precisely that: a condition—a state to which one is conditioned? Isn't exclusive heterosexuality also conditioned from the day of birth with those blue and pink cribs? Is one conditioned to "manhood"? Cannot a certain father be, in fact, a second mother? Was it not within a young male's rights to demand courtship privileges identical to those of the most popular girl in class? Could I too not be worshipped? Or was my role to worship?

Maybe the poet too is conditioned—even the first-rate poet. God doesn't make poets, parents do. In days when we believed in God, talent was not thought of as God-given but as a craft, a duty. Bach, Raffaello, were servants, it ran in their family. Today, with God gone, talent's an enigma, it falls from heaven. And gayness rises from hell.

Gay militants question my refusal to ally myself.

On the principle that I was among the first to come out of the closet (thereby, one might add, paving the way for their casualness in asking me to ally myself) they feel I'm now backtracking. In fact, it was never homosexuality but sexuality that I was open about. That the sexuality may have leaned in one direction is an unimportant assumption. The unimportance is the only importance which they should take from me for their propaganda.

I have never suffered from it. Perhaps I yet will, for who knows how the regime may end? But what I have become is not stamped with childhood trauma. I say this, of course, divorcing myself from stereotypes, with the safety of hindsight. Yet hindsight's all I've got.

Yes, I outwardly loathed macho sports, but did not—like textbook fairies—secretly wish to enjoy them; to kick a ball around a field was dumb, where did it get you? I loathed female sports too (what's the feminine of macho?), nor did I—again, like textbook cases—secretly wish to enjoy them; to sew fine seams seemed vain, how long would seams last? Oh, I did have fun making cakes and rather liked to swim, yet felt neither truly domestic nor competitive. Sure, I was a sissy (from where does the word derive? Assisi? sister?), but my manifestation of this sissyhood wasn't easily mocked. I was a composer.

"Passivity" was due less to shyness, a negative virtue, than to the built-in convictions of Quakerism, convictions buttressed by sensible and sensitive parents.

I did not suffer from the queerness of sex but from the queerness of being a composer. The suffering stemmed from being ignored. So unswervingly convinced was I of music, from the age of seven on, it never occurred to me that all other boys and girls didn't go home after school and write pieces too. My greatest astonishment came, and remains today, from learning that people don't care.

(Postscript on the athletes: Though I now express contempt, in the good old days they were gods, stupid gods in their locker-room ambrosia. Scared of the gods, how exciting I found them! But I did not admire them. The scandalous behavior of such gods! In religions more idol-oriented than Quakerism, God is a shocking example to us all.)

Circa 1949, I had just arrived in Europe and asked Norris, "How's the sex in Florence?" Shirley, overhearing: "You boys! You cross an ocean and all you wonder about is sex. Aren't there other wonders in Florence to interest you besides that?" No. The best way to learn a new language is in bed.

Jews can't perform French music. Born performers, they don't see that French music plays itself. Jews who do play French music well are really Gentiles who don't know it.

Jennie Tourel has no real notion of Poulenc; she *interprets* him, won't let him be. Since she's my favorite recitalist, I write it advisedly.

> ... *What think you? the grass*
> *grows everywhere, I must be a pansy*
> *myself, they say all the Jews are really*

wrote Frank O'Hara in *The Young Christ,* and was also wrong (if poetry can be wrong), since Jews who think pansy think goy.

If all the theater of our century disappeared except Terrence McNally's, future historians could still reconstruct the dramatic trends of today. McNally is so terrifically up-to-date, without himself being a trend-setter, that he would lend a new sense to plagiarism did not a wisp of his own float in at the last minute. That wisp is a national identity. *Sweet Eros* is too close for comfort to Fowles's *Collector,* but is saved by being a translation of English into American. *Next* is a rewrite of Ionesco's *The Lesson* with an American accent. If his earliest play, *Things That Go Bump in the Night,* was not exactly long by Robert Wilson's standards, its three hours were nonetheless massive, macabre, and O'Neillianly ambitious in the tone of the sixties, a tone one thought McNally would have played on more. But he turned with the times, grinding out broad farce upon broad farce, until with *Tommy Flowers* (a would-be parody of his native land copied from *America Hurrah!*) he became the crass chic hack that we now hear praised.

He seems in *The Ritz* to want to ape Feydeau. But *The Ritz* is not about anything, as Feydeau—or even Mack Sennett—is; it's not even about gay baths, since gay baths, like all sex centers, are humorless by definition. (A man can't hold an erection and laugh.) The script asks for wit, gets it only through performance, never through text. But it gives dumb straights a chance to laugh at gays, and dumb gays a chance to laugh with straights at what they feel is a self-portrayal. In three years this will all be as dated as *The Boys in the Band.* Meanwhile, though Terrence should have his wrists slapped, he does keep some good actors off the streets.

Rita Moreno is not among the good actors, being mechanical, shrill, lacking in any spark of the warmth that characterizes your standard fag hag, and playing Puerto Rican as

Stepin Fetchit played Nigger. As an actress she's capable of but a single stance: that of milking us beyond our line of duty. After each unfunny line, as the public breaks up, she preens until the laughter subsides. She needs the know-how of, say, even a Bob Hope, who claws through the guffaws to his next unfunny line. But then, McNally gives her no unfunny lines to pursue.

Because of its dreamlike anonymity the activity in a sauna has come to be compared to suspended animation. It is the opposite. To suspend animation is to jell life. In the sauna you suspend niceties of living, not life which is released full force. Because the force seems aimless, like toadstools which spring up anywhere, we esteem it nonreproductive. In fact, the force is no less indiscriminate than the helter-skelter sperm cells of heterosexuality. Everyone weeps after fucking, not from fulfillment but from pointlessness. How ugly, really, the rubbing together of even the handsomest bodies, the empty eyes unintelligent as pain, the fluids issuing vainly from the body which grunts in the smelly efforts.

Why aren't there more murders at the baths? Nothing could be easier: a quiet knife, a rapid throttle in the anonymous cubicle from where silence or squeals are the rule. Then again, Jack the Ripper killed whores instead of paying them. The most glamorous sadists have been poor; hostility stems from privation, or from an italicized notion of propriety. The baths cost a fortune.

What telepathy passes between the slave-master hate-love of black-whites? Does a master, by dint of literally possessing a slave, rape the slave? But that slave, by dint of being inherently physical, is more in a position to rape the literary master. Is this an inverted idyll? Do heterosexual white men long to be trodden by black women? Do heterosexual black men hope to be lashed by white women? Is not the carnalest sadism that which the weak perform upon the strong?

People are given to believing that an artist (or a homosexual, for that matter) is what he is by choice. Well, choice may be there on some childish level insofar as the vocation is practiced, but insofar as the urge persists there is little choice, and even less, alas, for the quality of results. Often I hear, "Why did you become a composer?" I *was* a composer. The question is, Why did I persevere? Perseverance comes from applause, for which the need *chez moi* is no stronger than with Casals or Schubert or the Curies who, despite loneliness and self-sacrifice, etc., were, after all, aiming at the target of their fellowmen. Without tangible appreciation—performance, publication, money, comparative fame—who would persevere? Nothing's madder or sadder than stacks of unplayed scores. And the unknown genius is anathema to our age of speed. Why am I a composer? To dazzle those virile paragons who bullied me in gym class. Have they noticed? But now the ball's rolling and it's too late to stop.

I've occasionally admired the Coctelian rightness of Truman Capote's off-the-cuff repartee, and for years have retained in my treasure chest of wish-I'd-said-thats the following from one of his long-ago interviews: "When I throw words in the air I can be sure they'll land right side up." This noon, thumbing the Goncourt journals, I came across this from Gautier: "I throw my sentences into the air and I can be sure that they will come down on their feet, like cats." The Goncourts themselves belonged to a race that could be called the Effete Heterosexual—the Straight Sissy—nearly extinct now, and strictly European, with members like the Duc de Guermantes, or Lewis Galantiere (who translated the volume), and almost a George Plimpton or a Peter Duchin, but not quite.

Whatever became of rough trade? Already in the sixties there emerged a type too sveltly masculine to be anything but queer, while the straight hardhat was too potbellied to be appealing. Today, after flower children, "passive" husbands, and unisex, one may well ask: If opposites attract, who is one's opposite?

Copulation is a limiting term in that it excludes sex involving less or more than two.

I am composing a cycle of songs for soprano Joyce Mathis, of whom a not inconspicuous feature, at least to me since I am white, is that she's black. I have chosen to musicalize poems only by women (I mention this now, and never again, since the main point of the poems is that they're good), but none of these women is black. For my music there are no good black female poets. More important, I can't identify from inside with blackness as I can with femaleness: none of my ancestors were Negro slaves, though half of them were women. Artists contain all sexes, but not all races.

Still, maybe Robin Morgan's harsh words years ago were true: "Leave Plath to our sisters, stick to men poets." If I feel no more need for Plath it's precisely because she *was* a woman, and I am not, not even metaphorically. (If I reject Sandra Hochman's plea for songs it's because her verse extols her own menstrual flow, not mine, and I can no more compose from within a bleeding female than from within a black one.) Not that a composer need *feel*, or even respect, a poem in order to set it well. And masterpieces which thrill are more impossible to musicalize than lesser verses that ring a bell. The question of which composers select which poets to set to music, and of how they set them when selected, is endlessly engrossing. A woman's setting of Plath might not be better than mine, but will be different, not only because she's another person but because she's female. How to prove that difference? Is there more difference between a man and a woman than between one good composer and another good composer?

It's hard to deal with a woman's poem insofar as that poem dwells on solely womanly problems. Yet I'm writing a cycle on women's poems. From Phaedra to Blanche, great-women roles have been written by men. But in plays, in opera, these roles have been part of a larger pattern—a pattern, however eccentric, we all grow up in. Could a man write a solo lyric poem, *as a woman*, and make it convincing?

On fixed scales we are prone to measure the realities of others by our own needs and experience, conveniently evading disparities of age, strength, class, even of era and intelligence. Did the smart lord of Gaul suffer more than the dumb peasant of Maine? Or, given absolute conditions, did the godly old Jew with his prayers suffer less than the young atheistic Gypsy who had no "belief" to cling to in the gas chamber? Widowed, knifed, betrayed, insulted, who suffers more, the wise Woman of Andros or the *Précieuse Ridicule?* And who can resist, or (dare one ask?) *learn*, from pain, while the pain is in action, and after the pain is gone?

If Solzhenitsyn's assertion were correct—that the liberty earned by our forebears is taken for granted by Americans who compromise rather than sacrifice to retain that liberty—then he is implying the need for an alternative before unworked-for freedom turns to chaos. That alternative is always violence, and violence is always war in some form. Now Quakers alone, of all intellectuals today, claim there is no alternative to peace. So they preach. In theory they practice. Freedom . . . from what? From persecution or from air conditioning? Sacrifice . . . what? Our children or our glibness? What comes of it all? Does the Belsen survivor, once reestablished in Israel, become more magnanimous, more "aware," than a solvent Kansas farmer? In saying that war accomplishes nothing I, in a sense, speak by rote, for I was raised a Quaker yet never suffered what George Fox suffered. Yet neither have I known the anguish of the Belsen survivor nor, for that matter, of Joyce Mathis, Ethel Kennedy or the checkout girl or Jean Paul Getty or my own sister Rosemary. But I am not a fool, my rote is not cant—is smarter than most—and I've survived till today.

The kindness of strangers? It is their hostility or indifference which scares, in supermarkets, buses, neighboring apartments. Daily I reach home in tears. Accomplishment is not a public calling card, fame is no armor, beauty is vulnerable, but dumb beauty's durable. To be intelligent yet to want to survive is the strongest accomplishment.

The song-cycle, *Women's Voices*, is two-thirds complete. A militant dyke asks, "What do you know about women's voices?" I'm forced to counter with: "What do you know about what I don't know about women's voices?"

Mediocre earth, if I don't judge others by myself, then by whom?

Daniken's premise is appealing: that Martian giants millenniums ago brought their know-how to earth, bred with "our women," thereby producing "a new race," then vanished. The only flaw is that species cannot interbreed, despite

their know-how. (Some species can mix—canaries with spar-
rows, donkeys with horses—and produce offspring, but the
offspring are mules, sterile. Other species can intermate—
gorillas and humans—but produce no offspring.) Even if
species could interbreed, one trembles to think of "our
women" impregnated by giants. But why assume those
"gods" had sex, or even two sexes? If they did have two
sexes, why assume their males came? Perhaps 'twas goddesses,
fertilized by manly earthlings, who, without more pain than
a sneeze, gave birth to the missing link.

How often are we told, not by artists but by critics, that
such and such a love story is weakened because the object is
not equal to the subject. We learn that Chéri's two-dimen-
sionality casts a shadow over Léa's credibility. That Murray
Head, in *Sunday, Bloody Sunday,* is a cypher hardly negoti-
able as common point of obsession between the two brainy
protagonists.

Now love, intense and jealous love, is always physical.
Since when must the beloved be "worthy" of the lover, or
vice versa? Brains don't couple with brains. Who says, for
that matter, that the philosopher is worthy of his call boy?
That the tycoon is up to his whore? Passion is brief. If it
passes but the love remains, the love turns into Great Love
wherein the carnal is never primary. (Obsessive love always
involves at least one young partner. Is there obsessive physical
—strictly physical—love which continues for years between
elderly people?)

Straight men get nervous because they always think you
have eyes for them. However, most straight men, like most
gay ones and most women and most everyone are physically
drab. Thus, after that initial split-second Yes or No by which

we all size each other up on first meetings, they should relax and go on talking about whatever people talk about. Still, they do worry.

Yes, I too am forever aware of, maybe swayed by, who here is old or young or sexy or not, or Jewish or too thin or swishy or too fat or female or rich or talented or useful, but I never *never* think about whether they're white (unless they're not) because no white person ever does.

Heterosexuals worry because homosexuals are demonstrably more promiscuous than they. The two reasons most often given for gay promiscuity are, one, since they exist peripherally they have no responsibilities; two, their one-night stands indicate an inability for fulfillment—a need to ceaselessly seek. Actually, the anonymous bang can be so totally satisfying that a repeat performance could only disappoint, like the same Cordon Bleu meal two days in a row.

Probably no heterosexual, no matter how well-meaning, can know what homosexuality "is," any more than whites know black. What difference does it make, since love has nothing to do with understanding, and understanding can even bring an end to bodily love? (Zeus and Hera quarreled, each claiming the other's sex was more capable of gratification. To prove the point they called in the hermaphrodite Teresias. "Who has more fun in bed, Teresias, man or woman?" "Woman." In fury Hera struck Teresias blind. In compensation Zeus bestowed foresight upon him.) The homosexual artist, in a sense, has the edge, since he or she intuits nuance, thanks to a lifelong immersion in a straight element. But again, vocabulary here misleads. Before Freud, or even just one generation ago, people didn't talk of, say, the "homosexual" plays of Shakespeare or Marlowe or Wilde or Wilder or Williams or Inge. No one, including the homosexual, has yet come up with a definition; and not one of the thousand homosexuals I personally know seems queer for the weary psychoanalytical reason of strong mother and cold father. Nature lets her chips fall everywhere, but whereas those chips fell upon precise terminology millenniums ago for women and Jews, in Lysistrata and Moses, only yesterday was homosexuality coined.

A drag queen pretends to be an extrovert woman. Mick Jagger pretends to be a drag queen. Now, although both are fantasists, neither is camp; camp presumes objectivity. Drag queens are quite subjective. Jagger's behavior is not homosexual, but nonsexual—a child in tantrums.

Gore Vidal and Paul Goodman are the only homophiles of their generation concerned with politics pure, that is, politics for freedom of homeland and for betterment of all people, as opposed to politics centering about homophilic justice. Cultivated American male homosexuals, at least before the recent revolution, were understandably carried by narcissistic interests on a road away from general politics. Even a European like Gide's dalliance with the USSR now appears like mere flirtation (although it was he, with André Dubois, a major statesman, who in 1940 organized the vast Franco-Jewish exodus).

Do not be too quick to understand me, said Gide.

Do not be quick to laugh at Shirley MacLaine's quip on the Awards show, "That was B.C., before China, ha ha," as she plays kneesies with enemy Sinatra just one week after her public declarations of clear-minded nobility. Her wanting it both ways recalls an interview years ago wherein MacLaine assured us that the emotional scenes in *The Children's Hour* were pure acting, since the very notion of lesbianism revolted her. Similarly Peter Finch, deriding the one issue he'd helped make sympathetic, claimed that the only way he could play those love scenes with Murray Head was by closing his eyes and thinking on dear old England.

As though acting were not just that: acting. Surely many of Garbo's gay leading men were capable of embracing her without puking. A gay man likes women, takes them more seriously, than does a straight man.

As Republicans see Communists in every woodpile, so homosexuals (like alcoholics), by a reverse procedure, see their own kind on every throne. But homosexuals in fact are mostly right.

Asked to sign a protest against UNESCO re denial to Israel of cultural stipend, I decline. Is not that declining a protest too? Can refusal mean anything unless publicly explained?

To be Jewish is to be what anymore? Once, alone among all people, Jews were doubly identifiable: as religious and as Semitic. No Jew I know is religious, and no Gentile I know thinks beyond being American. (Even I don't feel defensive about Norwegian origins.) What devil forever isolates and gets them so into trouble?

Changing heart, I phone back Lenny Bernstein to say okay I'll sign his protest. He asks how I could have thought of not signing. Intelligent people in the same milieu misunderstand each other as much as those in different milieus, or as stupid and intelligent people, or stupid people among themselves. The Tower of Babel is no assurance against solidarity any more than a common tongue nourishes compassion. There would seem to be no hope.

God knows gays are mostly dumb and silly. Almost as dumb and silly as straights. Yet to have homosexuality in common is probably more reassuring than to have a common language.

In 1948 I gave to Kinsey, who was then formulating notes for a book on sexual behavior in the artist, my observations about who "was" and who "wasn't" in the field of music, both creative and interpretive. The conclusions are noted in *The Final Diary*. Times change, and so does disclosure of practices. The one remaining invariable seems to be organists: 95 percent of male organists in America are homosexual, while 95 percent of male organists in Europe are heterosexual.

When revolution comes, humor goes and so does art. Art and humor, faculties for seeing three sides of the same coin, are reflections rather than actions and can be entertained only in leisure (in, ironically, the very decadence which was once thought to spawn inversion). The revolutionary, wearing blinders, must just look straight on to a single target. Which is why conservatives are everywhere more witty and more useful to the arts than are radicals. Radicals, like children, are unrelenting (the Apaches, for torture, turned over prisoners to their infants), softening up and looking around only after the fight is finished.

Camp, the native gay humor (ability to mock yourself before outsiders mock you), vanished from gayness when the revolution began ten years ago, just as docility and voluptuousness vanished as bromidic badges for women and for blacks. These insignias will never return.

Then does an old-fashioned haze hang over these notes? Well, they were mostly written before 1973. What dates seems less the substance than the fact of the substance—their need to get written. Urgency relaxes, we've all mellowed, the world still turns. Originally these paragraphs were sprinkled through a diary-in-progress, nesting incongruously among other concerns. Now melted together, will they jell? The general vocabulary (by which I mean the inescapable validity of every sexuality) is now part of the general consciousness and needs no plea. But the personal vocabulary which is mine—ours—answers to more fragile desires, some of which are uttered in the present paper.

Part Two

6·*Our Music Now*
1974

Musically speaking, America is the most vital land in the world, and also the most abject. Vital, because composition —music's so-called creative aspect (the first aspect by which the cultural health of a country must be judged)—has finally matured into model independence. Abject, because the dissemination of this composition, through performance and funding, is slow and painful.

The most representative American—unlike West European —composition is, for the moment, noncollaborative, specialized, and mostly for chamber groups (some quite large), usually without vocalists.

Sonic scenery, once named "incidental music," has not been an assumed appendage of our straight theater for years. I don't mean that compact medium called musical comedy, which thrives today, but "background" or "mood" pieces.

Economy, not taste, so raised the price of original incidental stage music that plays now use, when anything, canned sound effects.

Movies? No treatise is yet published on music's conditioning role in film. Bad music wrecks good movies, good music can redeem a bad movie, and any music can radically alter the intention of any given scene. Its "abstract" (though not neutral) force makes music more subliminally persuasive than any other periphera of film, something *cinéastes* have known from the start. Those handy pianists for silents grew up into the Steiners of talkies. Such studio employees—providers of auditory decor—gave way in turn to "serious" imports from New York. Then nothing. After the high-class wartime documentaries, movies produced no distinguished scores —no nonpop music with sufficient character to stand alone. Unlike stage music, which was priced into starvation, movie music depreciated with the advent of star directors, in Europe as in America.

Advanced directors employ hack composers, as though to join hands with a vital musician would constitute a threat. Or they too use the past. The famous concert accompanying 2001, for instance, contains not one original note (of course, by definition a movie about the future cannot use music of the future), while our breakthrough movies, which otherwise receive citations, content themselves with theme songs or straight rock.

There is no real collaboration in movies anymore. There is no stage music anymore.

There never was nor will be television music. Insofar as TV is not real-life reportage it is not TV. Any music heard (seen) on TV is less good than on a stage or phonograph, even music conceived for TV. The long shot is meaningless on TV. The closeup is TV's triumph. Closeups are arias. An opera made from only arias is not an opera. Even if it were, to present these arias as a series of closeups would be redundant. Consider the claustrophobia of *Scenes from a Marriage* —sung!

The appetizing possibility of opera conceived for movies, a format which may prove the salvation of the hybrid monster, has yet to be tried. Tried and true's what composers meanwhile persist in setting when not foisting upon us mixed-media propositions self-titled opera.

Barber's revised *Antony & Cleopatra* (on Shakespeare) will soon be granted a second chance after its sabotage years ago, although the new version remains Old Opera. Elsewhere the visual distractions of a Berio seem no more musically professional than in high school, and qualify as New Opera only because the composer calls them that.

If opera, even at its most outrageous, is distinguished from show-biz tantrums by the formality of its word settings for singing actors (i.e., by its superimposition of one set of symbols upon another set which will be interpreted theatrically), then only Stanley Silverman comes close to exemplifying the definition. His vehicles for real singers dadaistically amalgamate all styles past and present. They are small scale (dramatized song cycles really) and financially feasible for schools. Although they could be blown up for production in Tibet or Penn Station, they do not offer themselves as masterpieces.

Those still awaiting a composer of the Great American Opera find their chief candidate in Leon Kirchner. Kirchner, a maker of "abstract" chamber and orchestral works, is not known for vocal settings (if indeed he's done any), much less for lyric dramas. Yet during a decade his musicalizing of Saul Bellow's *Henderson the Rain King* has been the

loudest secret since *Who's Afraid of Virginia Woolf?* before
its unveiling.

Can Great American Operas be devised from Great American Novels? Previous chauvinist contenders have all been on
original librettos. Not that visible music can't be based on
preexisting literature (some think Verdi's *Otello* greater than
Meistersinger); it's just that American composers haven't yet
added convincing dimensions to classical European plays.
Or even to native blockbusters. (Britisher Benjamin Britten
with his *Turn of the Screw* and *Billy Budd* has, for whatever
reason, dealt more movingly than any American opera-maker
with preestablished American texts.)

Need for the Big Statement—still acute for book critics—
has become a thing of the past for most musicians, due
largely to inroads of pop where breath is short and inspiration collective.

Only two American composers have come up with memorable ballet scores in thirty years—that is, since the happy
postwar collaborations of Martha Graham with Copland,
Schuman, Barber, Dello Joio. They are Lucia Dlugoszewski,
whose concoctions for Erick Hawkins' choreography are a
hypnotic joy to both ear and eye (she herself performs on
instruments of her own strange construction, thus replacing
the late irreplaceable Harry Partch), and Leonard Bernstein,
whose accompaniments for dance remain paragons of theatricality even sans dance. Balanchine's caused nothing in American music.

No other serious composer has come so close to inheriting
that part of Stravinsky's specialness which allowed for the
staginess of sound—which asked that music be visual while
retaining its exclusivity as music—than Bernstein. But as
exception to prove any premise, he's not to be pigeonholed.

The most traveled composer in the world, he is the least cosmopolitan, his music, all of it, stemming straight from America's most identifiable heritage, jazz. Yet Bernstein is America's first Jewish composer, if Jewish, before meaning Semitic or Talmudic, means viewpoint. This meaning, consciously conveyed to his art, renders Bernstein's sounds and subjects more Jewish than those of, say, Gershwin and Copland with their Carolinian Negroes and Appalachian cowboys, or Hugo Weisgall and Marvin Levy with their Strindbergian and O'Neill heroines, or David Diamond and William Schuman with their fondness for Waspish symphonic forms.

And Bernstein is the only "classical" American who stays, in heart and in practice, a collaborator. Nine-tenths of his work is for theater (ballet, musical comedy, the ritual mass, movies) where he joins with others; when composing opera or a straight concert work he collaborates with himself.

There exists no more beguiling melodist. That this gift can be promoted not only charmingly but scarily is shown with a craft ever more distilled. His best piece to date, the *Dybbuk* dances, succeeds in conveying maximum Bernstein volatility through an almost silent tension. His niche in public fancy makes him—as such things are judged—our second most significant (although curiously not very influential) composer over fifty. The first is Elliott Carter.

From Stravinsky, Bernstein inherited the catholic virtuosity and Carter the grand-style fame. And Carter is the only composer in the world, not excluding Boulez, who could wear such a mantle with gravity—none other seems needed anymore.

How balanced with Bernstein's heat is Carter's ice! The difference between theatrics and dramatics. Bernstein is all civilized contrast, sentiment, narrative; Carter is monochrome madness, perfunctory, nonprogrammatic. Storytelling in Carter's music translates only as metaphor—as events occurring to instruments, not to humans. Such strictly instrumental occurrences sometimes cause this composition to be termed uncompromising. It eschews carnal appeal, nor does it presume to charm. Seduction in sound comes facilely through the admixture of orchestral timbres, through richness of color. Though Elliott Carter is skilled with that palette he is far more colloquial with intimate (though no less huge formally) conveyances. Except for the crimson human voice. Indeed, he most excels in that grayest, that most undifferentiated and, they say, most risky (because most exposed) and "pure" of mediums, the string quartet, for which few composers since Bartók have written with much sense of necessity.

Necessity, however, is what Carter projects. Not, as some would have it, the necessity of intellect but the clean-cut urgency of a child's fit. Like never-resting souls tangled in hell proceed his bowed counterpoints, and always performance after performance, *tangled in the same way*, like those viscous strands on a Pollock canvas which, actually still, seem yet to move through time. Nothing great is ever left to chance, and great Carter surely is in his ability to notate insanity with a precision which, after the fifth or twelfth hearing, renders the notes as logical as the placement of beasts in the Peaceable Kingdom. In the unwhorish communicability of the logic of folly (or the folly of logic) lies Carter's force, a force particularly intense for young citizens to whom personal grandeur seems again (after years of mindless group grooving) to be a need.

Or so I hear it. Clearly there's no such thing as understanding music, but one can misunderstand intelligently.

Our female composers are in all ways equal to their brothers. If Dlugoszewski is queen of the dance, Miriam

Gideon has for long decades been, in the cognoscenti eye, a weaver of vocal fabrics at once taut and tender. Her contemporary, Louise Talma, a more muscular craftswoman, is drawn to large instrumental expressions (although she's the only composer ever to have obtained a libretto from Thornton Wilder, the important *Alcestiad*, an opera yet to be heard in America).

No musician mixes more exciting orchestral hues or draws more personal melodic lines than does youngish Barbara Kolb, and none projects more purposeful know-how in vast formats than does Betsy Jolas.

Here are but five of a growing body of women composers. To single them out as such (deftly avoiding words like "lovely" which I often use for men) is maybe unfair since they no longer do so themselves. They do not wish your ear to recognize their efforts as feminine—as Ladies' Music rather than music. Nor really do they endure more discrimination than male composers; composers as a species are so foreign to mass consciousness—even to Music Lovers—that they go undespised in one amorphous lump. (Talma's opera remains unperformed not because she's a woman, nor yet a bad woman, but because she's a woman who writes operas.) Composers are all freaks, yes, but the public doesn't see them. What doesn't exist can't be scorned.

Conducting is visibly a domain of males. Fewer conductors hold good jobs here today than there have been presidents of the United States. Our country boasts less than twenty first-rate orchestras, and the women's committees who largely run these orchestras are not about to let any of their own claim such plums. Even American males aren't much in the running. With notable exceptions our conductors are foreigners.

In a gracefully talkative documentary on the trials of

America's sole female symphonic conductor, Antonia Brico, age seventy-three, shows herself more advanced sociologically than musically. Through all her lauding of sacred monsters like Schweitzer and Schubert we hear no word about any American performer or composer of either sex, nor even a passing reference to what we call modern music. Liberated women can remain reactionary artists.

The Russian cellist Rostropovich a decade ago commissioned a number of large-scale vehicles from composers all over the world. That he was also a great interpreter seems slight when you realize that, emerging from a creatively archaic country, he single-handedly caused to exist most of the important cello literature of this half-century. Imagine an American cellist, emerging from this creatively advanced country, pursuing such a notion! Or any of our virtuosos. No Cliburn, no Stern has yet—not even for his immortality—voluntarily paid for a new work, and those few big names who have, have through foundations.

Yes, Europeans are general practitioners and Americans are specialists in everything except recital song repertory. Young German or Italian or French singers master the problem of their native tongue first and foremost, learn thoroughly their country's vocal output, and often spend distinguished careers singing solely in their own language. Young Americans learn every language *except* their own. Graduation recitals feature songs in German, Italian and French, none of which the students "think" in; if they do offer an English encore it is tossed off with a fake foreign accent.

Due partly to the high majority of European teachers who deem English unsingable, partly to the opera-oriented bias of students themselves, the voice recital has atrophied in the United States. The students (those not aiming for musical comedy) sniff neither glory nor money in English-language repertory. They feel no pride in—have scarcely an awareness of—the long tradition of songs in English. To declare as they do that English is ungrateful is to see clearly the thrilling pitfalls which in foreign tongues are invisible. The only thing bad about English as a vocal medium is bad English. And the only bad thing about modern vocal settings is bad music.

A young soprano's most glittering model is unfortunately a Beverly Sills who, once she became a star in Douglas Moore's *Ballad of Baby Doe*, renounced both her language and her country for the rabble-rousing trifles of eighteenth-century Italy.

People in the Midwest imagine the Eastern marketplace to be congenial, homogenized. They ask a visiting composer for anecdotes about famous performers. He doesn't know any. Famous performers don't play his music so he has no occasion to meet them. He rationalizes that they wouldn't "know how" anyway.

Expecting her to reply, "They don't know what they're doing," I asked Barbara Kolb how the Marlboro contingent sounds when, exceptionally, they rehearse one of her not-easy pieces. (That contingent is, after all, drenched from birth to death in nineteenth-century middle-Europe chefs d'oeuvre, whereas Barbara is used to hearing her music at the hands of Fromm Foundation specialists.) "They're terrific," she answers. "They play it like music, not like modern music."

Finding myself on yet another composers' panel, our exchange becomes amiable prattle. The very twentieth-century phenomenon of the Roundtable on New Music suddenly seems obsolete.

There used to be mutual stimulation. Musicians of conflicting persuasions goaded each other about ideology. With cheers and sneers, flying fur and splitting hair, the identical questions and answers were spouted for the thousandth time. It all grew too loud, lasted too long and settled nothing, but it was therapeutic.

In the past years, simultaneous with revolutions in more urgent arenas, composers of quite different schools and aims have become live-and-let-live. They even play each other's music, because they are united in a sort of ho-hum defiance against standard virtuosos who ignore them. When they do join at roundtables their purpose is not to chastise each other but to present a united front before performing units. They want representation, copyright revision, their just rewards through royalty revisions, money from the government. To make these demands heard in high places leaves composers no time to meet on panels. They're too busy scribbling recommendations for each other to the National Endowment for the Arts.

Endowments. We welcome their encouragement, though it's touch and go. Certainly the trumpeted Cultural Explosion, if it exists, is independent of private or public sponsorship, and like most explosions exudes a residue of destruction and waste.

Lots of money is being misspent by self-appointed committees (like Fromm, the once noble) to determine Important American Works, the result to be funneled to conductors, here and abroad, too lazily busy to examine the music themselves. Both state and national councils of the arts require that not only unknown petitioners but also composers with long-standing credentials prove (in words and before the fact) that the music they need money to compose will be both a masterpiece and a profit-maker. Ford asks fewer questions, merely slashes the budget.

Foul times flourish. As though nearly all of us (including those who love it) were not already captive to rock's ubiquitous onslaught, WNCN, America's most serious music station (most serious in that, without too hard a sell, it services "good" music—much of it contemporary—to the largest per capita area), is, at this writing, screaming for help. Whether or not it is devoured by yet another pop-oriented policy, the much-publicized issue degrades all concerned.

Do these discouragements change the shape as well as the bulk of fine art today? Qualifications determine recipe proportions, not flavors. Sure, outside restrictions are bad, but limitations, whether imposed by an artist on himself or by the state, do not deter communication. Art is form, form is elastic. While remaining the same size and weight, form stretches itself grandiloquently to cheat censors. Censors anyway make less difference in art than in "life"—less difference to a novelist than to a journalist. For an artist pure freedom is dangerous, controls are good. But he must stay free to control his own controls.

Art does not grow from the collective tension of the left but from individual leisure. Sadly, our most liberal politicals are often the least culture-minded. Bella Abzug, for example, makes no statements on behalf of the arts, yet her district alone houses the most concentrated covey of first-rate creators this side of Paris in the twenties. God knows she's for human rights, but only the jaded rich seem to have time for the art of artists as well as for their campaign support.

Political art? Military marches impel men into battle. What marches impel them to turn around and walk away?

The next years may overhaul our awareness of serious national music. Every American composer has been called on for the Bicentennial and the results will be heard, like it or not, for a long time, on programs large and small in even the hickest towns. Already this year we celebrate widely the hundredth birthday of Charles Ives. Like Satie in France, our only musical primitive has become the most overrated of underrated composers, but his imposition on the general consciousness is wholesome. Except for Hemingway, greater America has always been a bit embarrassed by her high-culture figures. Now with an Ives festival, a Whitman bridge and a Gershwin postage stamp, we are finally making a thing of artists rather than of generals. The thing results from the responsibility of growing up.

Despite how Europe still sees us (as adolescent imitators, producers of, at most, Melville and Cole Porter), we start to view ourself intact. If, as the French would have it, we went from barbarism to decadence without an intervening civilization, our current afterlife, while it contaminates the globe on the one hand, on the other involuntarily, and slowly, slowly, sprinkles a rich and fertile pollen.

7·A Cultured Winter

Some art dates well, some badly, but all art dates, the worst and the best. From the moment he writes *The End* an artist's work becomes the past, like Bluebeard's wife. Even *within* a work of any scope, because time passed while he created it, an artist may have inadvertently introduced anachronisms; the sole purpose of his technique is to solder these anachronisms convincingly, to make them cohere in the flow of the work. The work dictates its own terms, whatever its location in the artist's catalogue or in the history of the century. Inspiration, of course, does not concern the artist. Even if it does, there's nothing he can do about it. Nor will a conscious timeliness in the long run make his work seem inspired. Certainly timeliness doesn't add to worth. *Lysistrata* and *The Trojan Women* may strike us as ironically pertinent to the present, but *The Birds* and *Oedipus Rex*— as great or greater—do not obtain to us at all. Paintings and movies from the 1930s are bad or good, embarrassing or thrilling, junky or skillful, but all are old-fashioned in both matter and style. Whatever period a work of art purports to depict, the work itself is situatable only in its own period. Jules Verne's visions of the twenty-first century are strictly from the nineteenth. Shakespeare's Cleopatra is strictly Elizabethan, while De Mille's Cleopatra is less involved with ancient Rome than with ancient Hollywood. Thus Bartók's *Bluebeard's Castle* is not "about" medieval mores but about the dawn of Freudianism in Hungary as observed through musical explorations of 1911.

So much of art is patience, merely patience, taking the time to do what others would never have thought of doing—not because it's so unusual but because it's so ordinary. Subject matter of itself need not be extraordinary. For every murder in Edgar Allan Poe there's humdrum heartache in George Eliot.

Movies

Fellini starts to pall. The characters finally have no ideas, just bodies. Except perhaps in 8½, where the hero poses thoughtful conundrums, Fellini derides intellectuals (poor Iris Tree in *La Dolce Vita*), and has now come quite to ignore them. So *Amarcord* isn't about anything. It moves not into but around Fellini's past because the actors have no extracorporeal notion. They eat and flirt and argue but there's no argument and so no target. Old Antonioni, Fellini's one-time competitor, used to make movies about duty. Insofar as he dropped his thesis (never having, maybe, realized he carried it) his films too have fallen. Still, the images of both men beguiled the unwashed, even some of the washed, and continue to render film not inferior but superior to the stage.

And what is great art? everyone sits around asking. Can

you prove that it's not conditioning? Ives and Vivaldi, Gesualdo and Crumb: Were we not told what to think, what would we think? Even Beethoven, who invented greatness (Bach never thought in such terms), is no absolute, since I for one reject his quartets as yardsticks in this conversation.

I've seen ten Antonioni movies over the years, some often, all with pleasure. Watching them, I've never been hotly concerned with what he was saying. Artists don't generally think "message" while working; message is added later by critics. (Or sometimes by the artist himself. In an interview Antonioni states, "This story reminded me of I-don't-know-what," then claims as a hasty afterthought that the "international situation" is reflected in his view of the story.)

Anyway, looking back, one does find similar emphases from film to film. Antonioni's best movies are about one thing: avoidance of responsibility. In the drama of loss, he shows the protagonists' inability to cope with, and their ultimate indifference to, the loss. Halfway through *L'Avventura* the fiancée, a major character, vanishes during a picnic; after a one-day search she is never mentioned again. At the end of *Eclisse* the devoted lovers make a date for next day (or is it next month?), and neither shows up. In *Blow-Up*, death itself is mislaid: the corpse literally disappears, without explanation, and no one is much alarmed. If the main human roles are good-looking, well-off, caddish types—types which Antonioni depicts better than he depicts working classes—his real hero is scenery: those bleak, breathing rocks, the trysting place now empty of tryst, the green green green grass ruffled in anthropomorphic breezes. The nonhuman elegance of buildings or of plants, like the wavering skyscrapers and smog-filled trees in *La Notte* and *Red Desert*, is still an elegance with personality—a personality that takes a leading role.

This leading role is nearly the only role in *The Passenger*, Antonioni's most baroque work, a satire of his traits. Despite a richly plotted script, context has edged out content; were it not for the constant low-key presence of Nicholson, decor would be the sole star. Loss here is not that of others, but of the self. Nicholson avoids a duty to his own past by relinquishing identity, by letting himself dissolve and literally die from the effects of life's "meaninglessness." Yet the portrait we retain is not of dead Nicholson on a bed, but of the hotel room which contains that bed, the dusty town square which contains the hotel, the squalid opulence of Iberia which contains the town square, the never-less-than-exotic earth which contains the land of Spain, and the thrilling, vicious God which spawned earth in Antonioni's image.

If Antonioni's movies are all about avoidance of responsibility, I state it advisedly. He himself says: "You Americans take me too literally." He means metaphorically. Like Cocteau, like Goodman, like any artist, he *is* literal: he intends verbatim what he says, and can only smile wryly at the "levels" of interpretation heaped over his work by us poor mortals.

Maria Schneider has no looks, no charm, no talent, and no intelligence. What do high-powered directors find in her? The music, as always with Antonioni, is nonexistent, except for a hint of source sound—the solo trumpet toward the end which evokes a sad bullfight. But like all big continental directors today, Antonioni is not one to let music flash uncontrolled hues over his palette. Indeed, there is not one first-rate composer in either Europe or America who is now writing first-rate movie music in tandem with a director.

I've always enjoyed Chabrol movies but not until *La Rupture* was I struck by how dumb they are. Which is not to put them down. But they do follow formulas which aren't intelligent so much as abstract: frames fitted around one actress, always the same, his wife. Film after film features Stéphane Audran in identical situations to which she reacts identically, icy in the heat, cold-blooded before hot blood. Of all his dumb films this is Chabrol's dumbest. Suddenly we find that Audran can't act her way out of a paper bag. Like Faye Dunaway, she is so wondrously fake, so fair of face, elegant of posture and so carefully posed, that we don't realize she is not "interpreting" but merely moving from stance to stance like a mannequin. But I'll buy her: she's a star who does know how to walk, which American women don't (question of actioning the legs independently of the midriff, and daring to take long strides). The film is too far-fetched for fear, and old-fashioned. LSD today seems so sixties.

Alfred Kazin made a smartish point about the insidious seduction of *Lacombe, Lucien*. Although moved by Malle's subtle virtuosity in showing almost every side of unchangeable human stupidity, Kazin found the movie's main premise false. He felt that though there may be banality to evil on the one hand, on the other people mean what they do and they act from conviction. Maybe. Yet Lucien had no conviction, he did exist, and he was a sort of *monstre* without being really cruel. He acted for approval rather than through common sense. If he confused obedience with betrayal, he was reactive to tenderness and carnality. Doltish but not charmless, a romantic Lieutenant Calley.

How the Festival Cinema selects short subjects is anyone's guess. I mention their current unfunny mime show, which patronizes the prose of Gertrude Stein, only because for humoristic purposes actual film clips are used of soldiers dying during World War I. A tasteless appetizer to a film about an artist concerned with life's values: Reichenbach's *Love of Life*, a movie on Arthur Rubinstein.

The theater's speaker system betrays the music, the distortion being most frightful during loud sections. A complaint to the manager brought this cordial retort: "Mr. Rubinstein was here for the premiere and *he* didn't complain." As though a guest would disapprove the menu when he himself is the chief dish. Of course, the film has nothing to do with music and everything to do with a musical personality. During ninety minutes not one piece is played through, and those samplings lasting more than thirty seconds are accompanied—lest we get bored—by melancholy landscapes or by physiognomies deep in thought. (In *Wuthering Heights*, a movie in no way about music, Landowska was allowed to play the whole of Mozart's *Turkish March* uninterrupted.) These predigested snippets glorify the performer over what is performed, a twentieth-century tendency which, as a composer, I deplore. (More of that later.) Still, the film is likable because it's an honest portrait of an honest man who is bigger than life without being aloof. Is it coincidence—Rubinstein's physical resemblance to Cocteau? More than any "celebrities" of recent generations, these two have seemed genuinely interested in other people. It's their gift of instant friendship, of making you feel you're the only person in the world. The gift can't be traded and it can't be faked. But it *can* be transferred to the silver screen, which quite melts into gold through Rubinstein's warmth and flows like sunbeams into the audience. That audience loves the hero not because he's a great musician but because he's a great actor— a pianist who also plays the role of pianist.

The film's all him, he dominates each frame. We're never sure to whom, off-camera, he's addressing those clichés about the soul, about death, about life and love and the pursuit of happiness. But the clichés ring true and are sometimes even touching because, though the pianist may be a ham, he delivers the goods. Although no artist, creative or interpretive, can ever make decent verbal replies to questions about greatness, we forgive the bromides Rubinstein utters with his lips, because he proves himself with his hands. We don't weary of his standard enthusiasms for standard works when his homely features crinkle into that infant grin.

As a cinematographer François Reichenbach is capable of only two stances: total anonymity, or total personality. The series he made fifteen years ago in an American marine boot camp was like a slaughterhouse documentary: individuals became symbols of the nonindividualistic military nucleus, and by extension of America as a whole, which is how the French still see our country. Meanwhile, in Reichenbach's TV portrait of Brigitte Bardot, no other human was permitted to encroach on the spectacular narcissism of the *étoile* who shone down upon us in her intimate glory as Rubinstein shines down now. When Reichenbach attempts to fuse these stances, as in his pornographic home movies during the fifties, he fails, for he takes protagonists from among people we know, and that leaves nothing to the imagination. The result is neither prurient nor informative. Reichenbach must be his own star, as in his socialistic documentaries, or his star must be the star, as in his personality documentaries. In either case he runs the show.

He is not musical in private life, but that's no disadvantage, at least in his dealing with a performing artist. (The best opera directors are laymen who realize that if action is properly spaced, music takes care of itself.)

Still, I shudder at how he might deal with a composer. What I deplore is not the film but the fact of the film.

Except for Hollywood fantasies in the thirties, or for rare documentaries (notably Madeleine Tourtelot's 16-millemeter examination in 1958 of Harry Partch's musical instruments, or the CBS television special in 1965 of Stravinsky as public figure), serious actual musicians canonized on film are always performers, never composers. A century ago, when executant and creator stopped being embodied in the same person, the creator lost out to the executant in both fame and fortune. Fame and fortune today do not lie in contemporary music. Performers who have movies made about them specialize in the past—Casals, for example, or Antonia Brico. A composer like Bernstein is filmed, yes, but always in his role as conductor or educator. It follows that Reichenbach should, and did, overlook one precious dimension of his subject: Rubinstein's service to living composers during the 1920s when he premiered works by Falla, Albéniz, Granados, Ravel, Milhaud, Poulenc, Prokofiev, Stravinsky.

Am I unreasonably jealous? Could one really film a composer *as* composer (the way Clouzot filmed Picasso in the act of painting)? Composing, finally, is a silent affair, forever hit-or-miss, boringly intimate, and not one bit visual.

Love of Life plays to a far different public today in New York than when I first saw it six years ago in Paris. Then it showed simultaneously in several theaters with long queues of young people waiting. Here it shows in one theater sparsely filled with immigrant septuagenarians.

For seven years in Paris Reichenbach and I led contiguous but unrelated lives next door to each other in Place des Etats-Unis. We went to different schools together.

Let's put in a bad word for the new National movie theater in Times Square, a sty that looks like a firetrap, a dubious site in which to see *The Towering Inferno*. Yet the owners charge four dollars a seat.

I dreaded this film, and it passed my direst expectations. I'm a good audience in that I'm unable to put myself above hokey effects: I believe what I see, and burn alive as the actors burn. But oh, the untheatrical attenuation of it all: it just goes on and on. There *is* a feeling of symbolism—those horrors momentarily represent our world's mistakes, and time running out. But the totality (and I do mean totality) starves us. Five minutes after leaving the theater I retained nothing, not even shock, not even annoyance, not even the trumped-up "message."

I've never been a fan of Paul Newman's acting, though I have admired his direction. Yes, he's gorgeous, smart too, and I'm in the minority. But he's embarrassing. That hammy boyish corny hard-earned vanity of our male actors! Newman, even in the fiery jaws of death, manages loving asides to the camera, and through it to his great loving public out there.

My only previous brush with the art of Mel Brooks was during the first half-hour of *Blazing Saddles*—before walking out in disbelief. Why were grownups laughing? Such wit belongs to the nursery. Once it was just Germans who laughed at digestion. (Americans laughed at sex, the English at money, the French at infidelity.) Suddenly we find not only Mel Brooks but an artist like Buñuel perched on toilet seats. Obviously I've missed the point.

Still, *Young Frankenstein* was mildly funny. Though one does abhor fans who coo too loudly too long, to show they dig each satiric reference. Did you know that the original Boris Karloff version was meant as satire? The cast split their sides during the rushes; no one was more surprised than they when the public "believed" the film. Today the strong part of that first version remains the lyricism. And in this new version one is more touched than amused by, for example, Peter Boyle's soft-shoe number.

Led to expect what we Americans consider "European intelligence" in the genre of *Claire's Knee*, I was disappointed. *The Middle of the World* is not intelligent, surely not in subject matter, which is romantic love, since love is *never* intelligent. There is a straightforwardness which Americans like to think is intelligence because they link it to the "frankness" of French cinema during our long night of censorship. Actually Alain Tanner's Swiss vision is bourgeois in context and devious in style (the willful quaintness of those 112 dated divisions!). It's less canny, less crafted, than, say, *Chinatown*, aiming a gentle focus on female repression. The background music, by one Moraz, is unintentionally comic. He seemed to be trying to write "sexist music," unaware that music doesn't have sex, though it can have preconditioned associations. For instance, all scenes with women and with love-making are awash with violas and vibraphones; all scenes with men in business conferences are peppered with arbitrary strokes on woodblocks and bongos. Very silly. One quickly gets the point, a point that hardly pierces through new meanings.

Books

Thumbing the galleys of Molly Haskell's voluminous essay on the treatment of women in the movies, with maximum interest and minimum irritation, it's stunning to realize how many movies she speaks of that I've actually seen, and recall like yesterday. Those I've not seen she evokes emphatically. The book's patchy and list-filled but that's neither bad nor good—diaries are made of the same stuff. Especially clear are her chapter on Europeans (has she lived in France?) and her remarks on Doris Day, who's my secret love (I even want to be Doris Day), but I could have used a little more Lana Turner.

Yes, I was annoyed by her facile, and now hackneyed, assumption about Albee-Williams-Inge heroines. It's unfair to draw conclusions re origins of female types in work by "known" homosexuals, especially when these conclusions can't apply to the females of, say, Noël Coward or E. M. Forster. She remarks on Visconti's "awe" of women because he's gay. But do their sexual preferences bear on the work of Cukor (the most famous of "sympathetic directors of women"), Vadim, Bertolucci, Tony Richardson, Carné, Hitchcock?

It does seem unbalanced to refer to the non-women of the Inge-Williams syndrome without once breathing the name of Cocteau in a book that purports to be inclusive. Jean Cocteau was not only the single most influential *cinéaste* in France (Truffaut, Resnais, Genet, Godard, Reichenbach would never have been as they are without him), and by extension in the whole "experimental" world since 1932, but a compassionately original creator of feminine roles. Think of those women of all ages and styles that Cocteau put on the map: Lee Miller (*Sang d'un Poète*), Gabrielle Dorziat, Josette Day, Yvonne De Bray. Or Juliette Greco in *Orphée*, or Berthe Bovy in *La Voix Humaine*—that most anguished of female roles. Even Jeanne Moreau owes to Cocteau her stage debut in *La Machine Infernale*.

Haskell gives Ophuls too much credit for *Madame de*, since the novel (and I think the screenplay too) was by Louise de Vilmorin, a powerful Parisian force and no fool, who also wrote other screenplays, and was persuasive *as a woman* in France for three decades. (Error of fact p. 238:

Le Amiche was the name of Antonioni's movie, culled from Pavese's novel called *Tra Donne Sole*. Here it looks as though *Le Amiche* were Pavese's title.)

   I still judge new works by whether they hold my interest. I couldn't stop reading John Fowles's collection, *The Ebony Tower*. The untried notion of the title story, bland on the surface, is finally perverse as all art. A youngish English artist and journalist, happily married and professionally "on the way," crosses the Channel to interview a famous old English painter residing in Brittany with two nymphet protégées. The old painter is reactionary, disabused, alcoholic, lecherous, inarticulate, egocentric, and a genius. The others are better-rounded, more idealistic, but lack the magic touch. "Ebony Tower" is the old painter's term for what has replaced the ivory tower: abstraction, escapism, fear of clarity; art is practical hard work, he feels. The younger man, overwhelmed after his brief weekend by the force of his host and the appeal—emotional and intelligent—of the young women, returns to his wife, destined to remain forever "crippled by common sense." The theme could never have been about composers: they just don't behave like plastic artists. Yet the symbolism—if one dare call it that—is of art in general: what works works; theories, though dazzling, can't inject life. The self offends, yet it's the crucial ingredient—it, and not good thoughts or smooth living.
   "Eliduc," the second story, a translation by the author of a tenth-century Lay of Marie de France, is a parabolic abbreviation of "The Ebony Tower."
   "Poor Koko" I read alone at night in bed and was scared (as I was of *Clockwork Orange*, which it resembles). Another allegory, though not very veiled, presented as the generation gap, but actually about the non-artist's resentment of the

artist. Since both representatives are here painted as medioc-
rities in their specialties, the crime and punishment—or the
crime of punishment—seem all the more gratuitous.

In the margin I wrote: "Like the *Marie Céleste*." In "The
Enigma" Fowles mentions the *Marie Céleste*. Surprise of a
familiar face—surprise at not being surprised! Fowles sets
up human puzzles for which there is clearly somewhere a
logical solution, but which, precisely because they're human
and not abstract, must remain puzzles until we ourselves can
climb inside. An algebraic equation has one possible formula,
human enigmas have many. Fowles is a true spinner of yarns
in that he sets up breath-bating detective-type givens. Like
Simenon his poetry is a lack of poetry (that is of poetistics,
of "fine" language). Unlike Simenon he presents no final
solution; paradoxically this seems more satisfying than the
endings to most mystery stories, which, being contrived and
deductive, are too logical for the always neurotic dramatis
personae. "The Enigma" is a sketch of society and country-
side. Fowles's depictions of the British—upper-class, pseudo-
left wing and official—are no less convincing than his Hamp-
stead Heath in the heat. Like Antonioni, he makes land-
scape into character, yet he's neither awfully imaginative nor
experimental. His writing contains a maleness which always
impresses but never thrills, always pleases but never soars.
These are not faults, they're identifications. Identity he has
indeed—his own clear, intelligent, recognizable voice. Yet
despite his excursions into medieval Provençal language, or
into the esthetics and history of the touchable arts, he seems
less intellectual than, say, an Iris Murdoch. Certainly less
philosophical.

The last, "The Cloud," is all first person and mostly conversation, "mood." Would-be sophisticated, and quite wearing. Doesn't work like *The Waves* or *The Sacred Fount*. And

the people aren't well-drawn. A worthy dud, but an unworthy climax to this collection.

Samuel Johnson has always skirted me. My parents doted on him (still do), and as a child I had a one-line role in a playlet about Johnson's Dictionary. But I've never actually looked him over, or even much of Boswell. That's because they seemed less artists than scholars, and scholarship's not my dish. So I am pleasantly surprised to be reading John Wain's treatise.

Part of the surprise lies in a continual misapprehension about the prose of poets. Always assuming that poets only write poems, I'm repeatedly disabused, and not just by Auden. (Look at the extraordinary recent essays of Louise Bogan or Howard Moss.) John Wain's prose is not one bit "poetic" but straightforward, researched, responsible.

His biography is a canvas of eighteenth-century manners on which he paints Johnson in a new light, free of Boswell's editorials. The lexicographer comes off not as the usual old-time Noël Coward, but as an old-time Edmund Wilson in all his feisty brilliance. I like the sketches of Johnson's wife, Tettie, of Joshua Reynolds, of David Garrick, of Lord Chesterfield. (Though I'm bemused at how Wain, without irony, tells us Johnson was incapable of bearing a grudge— this, after a chapter on Johnson's famous letter to Chesterfield—a three-page grudge.) And it is chastening to realize that poets, in social station and income bracket, are no better off today than yesterday. And to note that Johnson, as opposed to Boswell, was a comfortable liberal, outspoken against slavery and capital punishment and prison abuse. But there's little "clubable" talk of painting or sculpture, and none whatever of music. (Of course, there *was* no remarkable music in England then.)

The fascination of *Cockpit* is its lack of fascination. Persistent perversity can't add up, since each example is a retelling of the previous example, not a new slant or freshly growing layer. A theme but no variations, and always too doggedly heterosexual for my taste. Kosinski errs by claiming his evil hero to be a "symbol of our time," since any book reflects the time it's written in; the point must be made not through explaining but through presenting the protagonist. The author clearly has as much fun inventing his chilly anecdotes as Antonioni, say, or Fellini once had in creating their decadent capitalists, all in the name of righteous objectivity. But those films developed, like song cycles, whereas Kosinski merely collects, like this diary. He is a master of public relations, but his public product rings false and bears no kinship to craft. This is the fourth and last of his books I'll read, since each one is the same. Each book of Jean Rhys is the same too, but they all so nicely break the heart, while Kosinski merely steels the heart— and to what purpose?

Theater

Weaned on the premise that brevity is next to cleanliness, I have hitherto shunned his twelve-hour plays, so Robert Wilson's current stint came as a surprising joy. Three whole hours without a boring minute. Wilson is marvelous but not a bit new. Dozens of influences which one reacts to as to a happy synthesis.

He calls the stint *A Letter to Queen Victoria*—a fair title, since words are used throughout with syntactical sequence but never for literal sense. It's subtitled "an opera"—a fair identification, since music is used throughout, in conjunction with words, which, though not really sung, are rhythmicized and intoned. But the work is also choreographed: a ballet with speech. An opera without song, too grand for meaning, a soap opera. Indeed, most of Wilson's recognizable references are to TV serials and movie dramas, the way Cocteau's references were to Renaissance painters and Greek tragedies.

An introduction presents the actors. The curtain then rises on the first of four acts, each one self-contained and invariable, that is, of the same shape every night. Since every act—or separate play—has its own rules, but since these rules derive from the old trick of imposing non sequiturs as logic, any section could be longer or shorter to the same effect. In "abstract" ballets like *Sylphides*, the young films of René Clair, the plays of Ionesco or the music of Satie, time doesn't count: stretch it, shrink it, no harm's done.

Cocteau is everywhere. Part one, a discourse between two motionless women repeated verbatim at different speeds, reminded us (visually) of the conversation between Oedipus and the Sphinx in *The Infernal Machine*. Part two, in an aviators' prison (I think), where the actions of smoking and sleeping and dying are repeated verbatim at the same speed, reminded us of the Mexican execution in *Blood of a Poet*. Part three, all in a café where couples chitter-chatter and are interrupted only by an occasional gunshot which kills an actor and then another gunshot which kills a second actor but brings the first one back to life, reminded us of routines by Bob Fosse. Part four all dominated by an Oriental sage recalled dadaistic forays of Richard Foreman.

One binding force flows like the sands of time through these four parts: a pair of dancers who simply twirl, sometimes rapidly, sometimes scarcely. Unseen by the others, they yet remain always onstage, revolving with lowered eyes, never interfering, and like that monolithic slab moving through *2001* they represent pure motion, or, if you will, pure intellect.

Pure verbality, or, if you will, noncommunication on its top level, is represented by the very young comedian Christopher Knowles. Incorrectly termed autistic, i.e., unwilling or unable to speak, the boy is a verbose ham exchanging nonsense fugues with his mentor (Wilson "began" as therapist for the retarded. Therapist: The rapist). Knowles strikes you as very canny (retarded like a fox), as does Wilson's nonagenarian grandmother, who also plays a hearty role. What's unprincipled about putting these people on view? What's healthier than to be applauded for doing what you have fun doing?

The sets and costumes being always black and white like old movies, the only color comes from cheeks and hair and lipstick.

Music is omnipresent like the dancers. Composed, or rather, pastiched, by one Allan Lloyd, it parodies eighteenth- and nineteenth-century classics as counterpoint to the ultramodern doings on stage. (Again Cocteau: the film *Les Enfants terribles* and the ballet *Le Jeune homme et la mort*.)

If Wilson's theater is praise of inarticulateness—a communication, so to speak, of the fact that men don't communicate—then he has made a couple of esthetic errors. For example, at one brief point the dervishes, always mute in their constant motion, echo some talk from elsewhere on stage. This echo jars sufficiently to disqualify them as functionaries forevermore. And the music may well be willfully fake (fake Brahms, Schubert and Bach, fake Kurt Weill, fake violin exercises), but its function is real. It knits disparate elements of text the way Thomson's music lends order to the disordered verses of Stein. Now, music has the power for making any madness seem sane, or at least seem organized. Music is communication, and I'm not sure that's what Wilson is after.

On the other hand, Wilson never introduces the one normal protagonist (not himself, certainly) against whom the folly of the others may be contrasted. The zaniest satires of yore always provide an Alice, a Gulliver, as solid ground in Wonderland. Here everyone is crazy, except presumably the audience.

(He also mistranslates French. *La justice doit être entendue également:* "Justice must be heard equally." *Egalement* does not mean equally, it means also.)

To reiterate. Claims about Wilson are unsubstantiated, unless one translates avant-garde as synthesis. Wilson does not expand time like the Chinese nor contract time like the Greeks; his time takes the time it takes. He has not composed an opera, because no true musical mind is at work; the music is costume, not character. He does use words the way composers use notes, for sound rather than for sense. So did the Greeks. (Otototototoi. Keh Keh Keh Keh.) Indeed, many of his formal spoken canons as well as his paranoid outcries are traceable to Greek tragedy and comedy, while his personal tantrums are traceable to Beckett—not to mention Jerry Lewis, who did in public what we all wish we could do: acted crazy without being punished.

There's an elegant sense of scene: Wilson shifts people and things with asymmetrical taste, as Mary Wigman was wont, and his troupe is pleasingly rehearsed. If he is not innovative, he is personal, though I'm not too sure what his mythology is. He presents failure of communication as a symptom, but doesn't suggest cure the way more conventional playwrights do—unless the evening itself is a cure.

Though what does any art work solve? Solutions mean that conclusions are drawn, and art doesn't draw conclusions. Conclusions are finite, therefore pedestrian. Still, one usually senses what, in a general way, an art work is about, like love or war or death. Thus, if Antonioni is about responsibility and Molière is about hypocrisy, then Wilson is about communication.

His wit is close to Stanley Silverman's. But Silverman, as a composer, comes closer to composing actual operas—on Wilson's terms—than Wilson does.

How might he handle another's work? Leaving the theater we bumped into Kenneth Koch and went for coffee. I told Kenneth I was supposed to talk about Wilson on the telly, and spouted the pedantries I've just noted here. He listened with stupor. "You shouldn't be worrying about talking on TV. You should be worrying about how you can get Robert Wilson interested in our opera. He's the best director on earth."

Reviews had hinted that *The Misanthrope*'s updating lacked viewpoint. Why update, even with viewpoint? The best proof of timelessness—or timeliness—is to keep the work as written; let us identify with Oedipus, not Oedipus with us. (If, for argument, we agree that relocating a masterpiece is not injurious, why not play Beckett or Williams or O'Neill in Sophoclean or Elizabethan or Molierian dress?)

Still, forewarned is to be less jarred by modernisticisms. In this version contemporary references (pot smoking, De Gaulle, jazz) were superfluous, since the whole key is otherwise so stylized as to be acceptable as seventeenth-century. The one weird shift was not in text or scenery, but in direction—from Him to Her. After Molière's final line the curtain stays up while light fades on Célimène, alone and silent.

Alceste has gone, and we sympathize now with the predica-
ment of *her* future.

The difference between Tennessee Williams and Edward
Albee as users of language is that one is a poet, the other
a musician. Albee has claimed to be more influenced by
composers than by playwrights (which doesn't mean he's
more influenced by music than by theater); in fact, he never
personally knew any playwrights until he became—as we
say in America—successful, though he did frequent lots of
composers. Albee is a well-informed Music Lover, while Williams is musically naïve and tone-deaf. Both have utilized
moody musical decor for their less naturalistic plays. But
when it comes to adaptations of their actual words for
singers, Williams lends himself admirably to song and opera,
Albee not at all. Williams' prose, being poetry, is easily set
to music; Albee's prose, being music, is impossible to set to
music.

Albee's prose is musical, not through images (which in
his case are seldom flights of fancy, but pedestrian halts)
but through rhythm—the use of echo, balance, pause. If
meter defines his style, his content is charisma flavored with
vitriol, that is, with mean personalities more agile at anxiety
than at idea. When these elements mesh, they crackle and
satisfy onlookers.

In *Seascape* style and content seem at odds. Quips which
in another setting might get chuckles now fall flat when
asked to be taken frankly. The first act was nicely boring,
the way a Haydn duet is boring. I was soothed and pleased
by the series of waits, the canonic entries; it didn't matter
what the two characters actually said—their banality was
eloquent. Still, the first act fails because, being all style, it
is strictly a setup for the second act, and as such could have
been trimmed down to a brief prelude. The second act fails

because, being all content, the ideas are so sophomoric. The two acts should be joined and made, so to speak, into straightforward fantasy (pure comedy). Here we're offered a delicate appetizer and a leaden dessert, with no main course to justify the two.

JH feels that Albee's weakness lies in avoidance of characterization. A Williams drama, even at its purple worst, always shows wounded or laughing individuals moving through the mismanaged argument. Because they are individuals they lived (or died) yesterday and last year too, and are brought back tomorrow and next year by their maker in other plays. They people his *oeuvre*. But Albee writes plot before personality. At his recent best, *Box Mao Box*, the actors are still symbols, mere musical symbols, and we are depressed to realize they will remain forever unchanged. There is nothing, as the saying goes, of Love in them. Even the realistic Martha and George are not persons. Plays can't be symbolic and last. Not even Everyman.

There's something funny about talking of "Albee" and "Williams" as though they were stone figures rather than old acquaintances. As though I didn't actually know them. In fact, I don't know them, I *knew* them. Even a lover or child or parent, lost for a decade, becomes unrecognizable.

If indeed brevity is next to cleanliness, then *The Taking of Miss Janie* is the cleanest show in town. Now the virtue of brevity is highly professional, but it's a form of form, not of content. Indeed, this play has little content, less language, and is so dependent on our need to see wryly the recent past from a vantage of the immediate present that this device will itself seem exhausted a year from now. But tonight the form clicks.

The subject, such as it is, is that *cliché* is no less a black weapon than a white. Literal-minded as I am, I began by taking the drama at face value, aghast at its fund of non-dimensional black-and-white blacks and whites. Not until halfway, during Lonnie's monologue, did I sniff the satire. (The reverse occurred at *Easy Rider*. I rather enjoyed it until I slowly realized it was no takeoff; everyone was taking these hip bromides very seriously. From there on I loathed it.)

I like Bullins' large garland of what can only be termed songs: each actor has his solo in the spotlight, and each, though stereotyped, is complete and differentiated. I also like the staging, as in the tableau of Mort on the floor, blood oozing from his lips, while over on the staircase Glossie applies lipstick.

However the basic conceit is too unusual to be left unexplored. Who still accepts the old saw about "Love to friendship never"? One constantly sees passionate affairs evolving into workable nonsexual ones; but that a platonic relationship should, after ten years, turn to rape is not believable. Rape is an anonymous single-minded compulsion: it just can't occur between friends. Or if it can, the audience deserves a closer squint at the pathology. (This was the incredible mistake of Hitchcock's *Frenzy*, and to some extent of Chabrol's *Le Boucher*. It is the anonymous whore, not the dearly beloved, who risks the attentions of Jack the Ripper.)

To the circus with JH. Gorgeous tigers without expertise. The rest was sordid, perfunctory, with neither adventure nor surprise. Hard-sell, patriotic, mirthless. Childhood recollections of the circus are thrilling, yes, but sad. I used to ponder the love life of that tight-knit family. Today there's no sense of camaraderie, and it's not just because we're grown up.

The children didn't seem elated, the Garden was half filled, microphones conned us at every turn with televisionisticisms. As for Philippe Petit, the notorious *trapéziste*, he lacks eroticism, vulnerability, métier.

The Wiz. What to say about something so alien to what I think of as fine? Although like the circus it makes no pretense at being other than a money-maker, the genre of canned laughter is disinteresting, and the amplification of every laugh is *dangerously loud*. For someone partial to understatement, *The Wiz* is lousy: lousy music, lousy words, lousy vulgar vaudeville gags, and the cast, without exception, lacks winsomeness, as one thinks back to the perfection of *Carmen Jones*, so darlingly based on the same gimmick.

In *I Am a Woman* Viveca Lindfors remains handsome, with a continental carriage that works fine in drawing rooms. Her problem is that she can't act. Considering she's barnstormed in the show and knows it cold, how can her evening be ungraced by a sole professional minute? No diction, no projection, no differentiation between roles, and the too-frequent distracting mannerism—a curse also of Cher, Natalie Wood, and many another long-tressed thespian—of combing her hair out of her eyes with her fingers.

We the audience become a collective retina, the accumulation of dozens of pairs of eyes. Concentration is extreme, for we have *paid* to concentrate. We catch all gestures and assume they mean something. To learn that a gesture means nothing is to be had. We are disconcerted when it is replicated in every one of her multifaced monologues, for the gesture (which we hoped was Plath's or Freud's or Nin's or Lear's) is only Viveca's, sucking us into her ego rather than into her personification of another's ego.

Music

Music, by its so-called abstraction (its absence of literary meaning, which thus paradoxically gifts it with infinite meaning), becomes a flexible power, and very tough. If in movies and plays where it is used secondarily—that is as background—music can't actually make or break a scene, it can certainly set a mood and even change an author's intent from, say, sad to glad. By the reverse token, in opera, where music is primary, the composer's intent is hard to sabotage by even the willfullest mind. Still, in their infinite wisdom directors often do their worst to "illustrate" music. Béjart managed to make both Berlioz and Stravinsky sound measly in the garish shade of his misrepresentations.

More recently Zeffirelli, hired in 1966 by the Metropolitan to open the new opera house, nearly killed not only composer Samuel Barber but Shakespeare himself by infecting them with elephantiasis. At the premiere the stage's giant turntable was permanently broken beneath tons of tulle, Roman armies, live goats, and even camels. The blame, as always, fell unjustly on the composer who, disgraced in fortune and men's eyes, produced little thereafter.

A second chance for a new work which fails the first time is risky and rare, at least within the same generation. It occurs sometimes for a play—Tennessee Williams' *Milk Train*, the year after its New York flop, was refurbished and thrust back upon the same city the following year—but never for an opera. This precedent has now been broken for Barber's *Antony & Cleopatra*. Nine years after its flop at the Met it has been revised and reheard successfully at the Juilliard School.

Stripped of its "camelflage," the new version is improved through minor additions, major subtractions, a straightforward set, Menotti's tentative mise-en-scène and a cast of youngies who, as actors, are no worse than most singers. We can now judge this opera for what it is.

What it is is no closer to Shakespeare than the Shakespearian excursions of Verdi, Berlioz, Tchaikovsky, Prokofiev, Britten, Debussy and Diamond, but it is close to Barber at his most deliciously skilled. The overall sound is hyper-romantic out of Glière via Elgar and Hollywood soundtrack, while the thematic substance is never less than serviceable and sometimes rises high, especially when the texture is leanest, as during Antony's long suicide scored just for kettledrum and flute. The dramatic sludge is the fault of a play which is more political than amatory. Lovemaking verses had to be borrowed from elsewhere (the duet "Take, O take those lips away") and sound inappropriate to this pair of middle-aged politicians.

The total, almost nose-thumbing, eschewing of novelty seems itself novel—an experiment in the bland. But Barber's vehicle also is touching and large. It deserves to stay in our part-time repertory as much as, for example, the various Janáček revivals, because it is the last American opera in the grand tradition.

Stanley Silverman's new little opera, *Hotel for Criminals*, needs the witty energy of his *Elephant Steps*. Pastiche and parody are legitimate expressions and can be funny. But this is pastiche of pastiche (the dadaism of Buñuel and Clair), and parody of parody (Satie and Weill). Imitation of imitation provides no nourishment; one goes off hungry.

Silverman's mimicries are too near for viewpoint, and thus for caricature. The literal quotes (from *Sacre* or *Pierrot*) are literal for no reason. Parody usually has focus. The unique voice of Gilbert and Sullivan gleams through their pseudo-Rossini, but we don't hear Silverman through his pseudo-Satie.

Went last night to hear Lucia Dlugoszewski's *Angels of the Innermost Heaven*. On the same program were George Crumb's *Songs, Drones, Refrains of Death*.

The vogue for Crumb is dumbfounding. That his six effects in search of a mind should appeal to the vulgar is comprehensible: disembodied colors shine bright. That the effects should pass unquestioned by executants is also understandable: anyone can produce them and they get a big hand. But that critics should fall for it—should indeed have created the vogue—is as depressing as the toadying by the cream of P.E.N. to Yevtushenko a few years back (though Russia's Rod McKuen, as an alien guest with political principles, extrapoetical though they may have been, did bring extenuating terms).

There is something subversive—worse, hickish—about Crumb's persistent setting of García Lorca's Spanish, mooning on each big-scope syllable of *muerte* or *luna* with a meaningless meaningfulness that must sound silly to native ears. If his music had some Yankee viewpoint! But it exudes mere memories of Falla.

Many a great work remains great for my mind, though my body rejects it (the *Missa Solemnis*, for instance, or the *Goldberg Variations*). Even my mind concedes no greatness for others (Schubert's piano sonatas, the Berlioz machines). Crumb's language depends on what was a speech defect *chez* Varèse. The language is neither interior nor exterior, but gimmick. Assembling the tassels of fifty years ago, he's made his main dress, adding associative titles and literal quotations. But who is *he?* The Vonnegut of music.

Admittedly Crumb has "reintroduced" expressivity to avant-garde concerts, which comes as a quaintness to blasé ears, but his music is nothing *more* than expressivity—hanging unqualified in air. And admittedly I'm resentful, as is Lucia, her brief rich piece for five clean brass being as crimson as the Crumb was gray. For thirty years now Lucia, on instruments of her own concoction, has (like Harrison and Partch, without benefit of Iberian verse) fabricated sound worlds as personal as Crumb's are derivative.

Where in five years will they be? But their oblivion's no consolation to the me of five years hence. Various revolutionaries may well banish ageism as indeed they chant the rights of children, and by logical extension force sexual privileges upon the dying. Yet few heads turn when now I pass, and who will want to own me when I'm dead?

By pop standards Anita Ellis' nightly concert at the Birdcage is old-fashioned, and so is her vocal style. But everyone loves her because what she does is now rare, and she does it better than anyone.

Her platform manner is without manner. She stands there and sings, in basic black. For occasional emphasis she'll raise a hand like Lenya, close her eyes like Billie, or throw back her head like Piaf, but no histrionics, no sequins, no flailing arms. She's motionless, but what emerges is hot with action. She can shift from a whisper to a roar and back again in the space of three notes and not sound wrong; or hit and hold onto a tone, making it melt from an icicle into a tear merely by increasing her vibrato. The trick echoes Streisand and Garland, but Ellis was *their* big influence: she coined hysteria as a vocal art.

She herself claims to being influenced by, of all people, Fischer-Dieskau. One does detect more than a residue of black women, though all her material is by white men. The selection is small (she's been doing the same twenty songs for thirty years) but classy: handpicked bonbons from the stores of Kern, Arlen, Wilder, Weill, or from sound tracks of movies she dubbed for Rita Hayworth.

If the repertory of Anna Moffo is deeper than Anita's, Anita is not necessarily the lesser artist. American opera stars could learn a lot about English diction from her. Pop singers do have it easier than concert singers: their vocal range is narrower, they profit from the intimacy of microphones, and their words—"lyrics"—are simpler than the poetry of recitalists. But recitalists too often rely on beauty of voice at the expense of projection of their not-simple poetry. To need to stress that Anita knows what she's singing about is to decry the absence of what would seem to be the obvious goal of singers in any category. (Rock singers have nothing to do with singing, but with recording.)

With pop singers, it's not the song but their way with it. The difference between pop and classical is the difference between playing and what's played. Jazz is a performer's art, classical a composer's art. With vocal jazz, pleasure lies less in what's sung than in how it's sung. True, Billie Holiday did certain good songs often, but she also had a knack for making trash good, for bending tones until the tune became hers. We have *arrangements* by the thousand of pop songs, while songs by Schumann or Poulenc can't be "arranged" and still retain identity. Pop is variable, classical invariable. A classical piece exists in a unique state, there is no question of fooling around. Insofar as a singer takes liberties with a classical song its composer is betrayed. (Insofar as a coloratura *colors* a *bel canto* aria by inventing ornaments to hang on the written phrases, she steals the music, as jazz artists do, and sometimes improves it.)

I've never heard a singer, no matter how proficient, who was convincing in both "kinds" of music—pop and classical. Opera divas have enough trouble scaling down to Schubert songs without adding their hokey rolled R's to Gershwin tunes. As to whether an Anita Ellis could handle an opera role is beside the point; that which is *hers*—the crooning purr, the world as cameo—has nothing to do with arias.

Coincidence this morning delivered the disk *Classical Barbra*. Once I wrote that Streisand could handle certain arias if she wished, but her timbre is geared in other directions. (By the reverse token Grace Moore, more recently Eileen Farrell, just never had it when trying to swing.) The point now is demonstrated by this record, starting with the title. Except for the Handel, none of her "numbers" are classical—they are what *l'homme moyen sensuel* thinks of as classical. Streisand's error is to aim at her mass public rather than to put out an edition for just a few thousand dear friends.

The program note boasts that "only one song in the collection is sung in English," as though classical meant foreign, arythmic, and as though beat or color betray pop leanings. Now, these songs contain a wider expressive range than pop songs, both in tune and text, yet Streisand feels that's exactly what "classical" songs don't contain, for classical means restraint. (Respect without comprehension. No language talent. No musicality, considering how musical she elsewhere is. Etc.)

Argument with JH about whether the two musics will ever be one. He feels that *au fond* they fill the same need, I feel they don't. If they did we'd have the same music. Pop music is erotic, while church music, by removing rhythm, no longer resembles sex. (But who can say what's sexual?)

The fact remains that, in our century, although some instrumentalists live by playing in jazz bands at night and symphonies by day, and although some classical "vocalists" can skillfully warble pop, pop singers simply haven't the tools for classical. (Imagine Holiday or Bessie Smith or Peggy Lee convincingly faking even the dumbest Donizetti, let alone Schubert or Poulenc or Christmas carols.) Those with technical equipment miss the point, like Streisand.

Two kinds of music have run forever parallel. Call them sacred and profane, church and folkloric, classical and popular, indoor and outdoor, high and low, isolated and participatory, specific and general. They have always had two definable audiences. Only in recent decades has confusion arisen, a rivalry, a sense of either/or. High prices granted to entertainment industries have allowed these industries a high notion of themselves and thus to feel they're where it's at, they're what the public wants. They're right. But what public? Once upon a time the distinction of entertainment lay in its passive public, while art (even the simplest) presumed some activity from the audience, a willingness to come halfway. Things blur in today's heterogeneous world; good and bad are thrown at us in look-alike packages.

Lukas Foss is a triple threat: composer, conductor, pianist —and more than just first-rate as each of these. He's also an organizer. Five years ago he took over the venerable Brooklyn Philharmonia and concocted a series of marathons: six hours of one composer or of one period performed to satiety— sometimes several programs occurring simultaneously in separate halls. Occasionally the marathon is of strictly contemporary music, a subseries called "Meet the Moderns."

It was to the most recent of these that I hied me last week —a three-ring circus on a weirder plane.

The Brooklyn Academy is harder to find than an elephant graveyard which it's about as cheerful as. It contains a suite of gloomy rooms and stairways around which have been constructed three vast ugly concert halls with sharp acoustics. In these halls four separate full-length concerts were presented. Three of these featured an international cast of every persuasion. For Lukas is nothing if not catholic. Five years ago various "schools" of composers warred with each other; today they often share the same bed without complaint.

While three concerts were being presented consecutively downstairs, a fourth was presented simultaneously upstairs. This consisted of one work, John Cage's four-hour *HPSCHD* (pronounced harpsichord), for six harpsichords and mixed media.

If not the best, Cage's was certainly the most famous piece of the evening because it lasts so long and costs so much. I'm not quite sure what *HPSCHD* is for—what we're supposed to *do* while experiencing it—but it's embarrassing by its *déjà vu*, a quality not found in even the most conservative of the other pieces. I gave it as much as my eardrums could afford (about eleven minutes).

Of the many pieces I most enjoyed Gregg Smith's settings of Blake, smooth French vocal writing unblushingly lush and very charming; Jacob Druckman's *Valentine for Solo Contrabass,* a short witty piece played not with a bow but with a drumstick by Donald Palma all in black looking suave against the dark red of the huge instrument, and very charming; Englishman Peter Maxwell Davies' *Missa Super L'Homme Armé* with its amusingly unhip British jazz and theatrical whoops, all very charming (although his practice of having the singer declaim rather than intone the Latin verses is not a musical solution to the problem of presenting text); and Wuorinen's *Speculum Speculi* for six disparate instruments, which, despite a certain spikiness, was also kind of charming. Charm, indeed, was the keynote, even of Cage's piece. And although the crime of charm ten years ago was punishable with exile (and even today the word makes these living composers turn in their unquiet graves), surely charm—by which I mean color for its own sake—is what attracts the young to these works.

Though there weren't many young, or many anyone. Those who were were devoted and stayed to the bitter end.

I did not. It grew late, so I skipped the panel of composers which was the postlude. However, I've heard most of what composers have to say, and learn less from what they say than from what their music says—except for John Cage, whose arguments *are* his music.

Cage, like most household utensils, gets rusty and needs resharpening from time to time. His arguments grow lax: he justifies poetry with poetry, thereby stopping conversation. When we say it's just noise, he quotes Cummings: "In just spring . . ." and asks: Is spring just? But assuming Cummings had a meaning, "just" can mean: "mere," "only," "deserved" (just rewards), "fair" (he's fair and just), "exact," "specific."

A throw of the dice if a piece is to be long or short. If it's long, we the public must accept this, though when the piece is over we're closer to death than we would be if the piece had been short. We have made a gift of time to the whim of dice. Of course, any decision bites moments from time, including the decision to say these words.

It's not by chance his music of chance is better than other people's. During Cage's piece people didn't do anything except look around as though they'd missed the boat. They did not, for example, lie down on the floor and screw.

People always used to ask, "What do you think of Cage?" or "What do you think of Menotti?" Today they're facts of life.

If Cage proceeds on false presumptions (namely that noise is music if you know how to listen) his explications are always winning, which is why the question-and-answer period is the best part, and may indeed be the most musical part, of his evenings.

If fundamentals of music composition were taught in the nursery, people wouldn't say—as they seldom do about pictures and poems—"I don't know anything about it." Music is not inherently mysterious, but education makes it so, and without guilt. Which is why musicians can usually talk decently about literature or painting or plays, but authors and painters and playwrights without flinching change the subject when music's brought up, unless it's rock.

If less is more, then conversely more is less. Yet there seemed no offense in the old-fashioned length of all this, because of the nice variety.

I was amused Sunday by Walter Kerr declaring, "We don't *need* revivals." That's precisely the contrary to what music critics are permitted to say. Nine-tenths of what drama critics review is contemporary; nine-tenths of what music critics review is a century old. Plays, in principle, have runs, and so can be discussed as something for others to go see; musical events, in principle, are one-shot deals, and so must be discussed as obits—as passed occurrences. Exceptional, then, are two events attended last week. Shakespeare's comedy is the revival of a past occurrence, while Boulez' concert was of thoroughly new music. (Nonetheless, that new concert itself is a past occurrence, while the old play continues to recur in the present.)

Boulez has been for thirty years not the *enfant terrible*

but the intellectual conscience of music. His early works were eerily reasonable in their avoidance of easy sensuality, and his creative influence was nothing if not a triumph of style over content. He did not flirt with the ear, and it was with the eye that we examined, on paper, the labyrinth of his processes, processes worked out for piano solo or for instruments of one family where color mixtures could not take precedence over profile. How radiantly simple, how expressive, how even gentle his new music seems. Of course, we're conditioned by knowing his old music. But he's no longer redoubtable; his reason now lies in his lack of reason —in his stress on sonority right in the tradition of French impressionists. *Eclat*—sparkle, burst, flare, chic—is all that. Boulez here uses instruments for their own sexy sake, choices not of logician but of alchemist. Splinters of brass and copper fly from mandolin and cimbalom, and resolve themselves in our ear as perfect gold. But don't tell him that.

Joseph Papp's *Midsummer Night's Dream* embarrassed me. I've been thinking how I, who never go to the theater, have seen this comedy over and over. It's one of the first plays our parents took us to, when Max Reinhardt came to Chicago with Mickey Rooney. The movie of same. Then at Stratford-on-Avon in my adolescence, and later the ballet *Les Elfes*. There also have been Britten's magic, most recently Peter Brook's pedestrian, versions.

Shakespeare doesn't need us to tell him what a pretty piece he wrote, but how would he take these amateurisms presided over by a Puck like an MC in a Harlem gay bar? The actors have no talent, no charm, no physical appeal, and no ability to speak English comprehensibly—much less with grace. Not that Shakespeare is sacrosanct, but he should be taken away from Americans forever. We lack the gift for dealing with his elegance and with his farce, or indeed with any drama removed in time and based on speech rather than on visuals. I'm not against colloquial adaptations; Shakespeare sustains them. But even in his day, the speech of his plays was not daily parlance but versified and rhymed, and the eloquence was that of a poet, not a peasant. Our actors do not begin to know what they're speaking.

Dance

"I try to hold up the mirror," says Alvin Ailey, "although I try not to be too depressing about it. . . . I'm against racism . . . but I think we have to get together—and dance together. I like to celebrate the difference. . . . I choreograph because I think dancing is beautiful." Like most people of the dance he doesn't intellectualize, and avoids specifics even when answering what he calls "flack" from black militants.

Well, I revisited the company and found that, although there's no racial integration, Ailey does hold up the mirror to his own featureless claims and tries not to be too depressing about it. The program reconfirmed a derivative focus with commercial spirit. *Night Creature* uses one of those sprawling rhapsodies Duke Ellington loved to confect: long as the clock ticks but organically short, being bits sewn together. (Like Gershwin, Ellington longed for symphonic "legitimacy," but his Big Statements were less convincing than his straightforward blues.) Ailey's dance steps are cheery, graceful, Gene Kellyish, nothing much.

Portrait of Billie, for two dancers and the discs of Holiday, was designed sixteen years ago by John Butler (who, of course, is white). How be fair about it? Billie Holiday is someone whose fans get proprietary. Since childhood I've been one of them, and can't help feeling that any interpretation of her, beyond herself, is forgery. Billie's songs are so strongly self-contained that to watch her danced to is like looking at a painting through a stained glass window. Each of the four dances seemed to exhaust itself before the four records were over.

Feast of Ashes, choreographed to Surinach's lean kinetic throbbings, is a dead-serious version of Lorca's *House of Bernarda Alba*. It stars the house star, bizarre Judith Jamison, who, with her long long appendages, kicks a lot. Indeed, Ailey's creative gamut extends from showing pleasure solely through a finger-snapping shimmy to showing pain solely through kicking. Judith Jamison is not actually *used* here any more than she is used in the final *Revelations*, a series of dances to spirituals sung by a mixed chorus in the pit, mostly a cappella, but occasionally accompanied by percussion, more Cuban than Black Slave, sunbursts and white chiffon, Billy Graham via Radio City. This is Ailey's most popular ballet and it's pure showbiz. Like Terrence McNally's exploitation of queer jokes for the delight of straight hicks, Ailey is falsest at what he presumably knows best. His black scene is about as kosher as the edition filtered through white *boîtes* in the twenties.

None of this would make the least difference were an inventive force at work, some sense of need. The corruption lies not with the dancers. You *can* know the dancer from the dance. Excellent performance, far from camouflaging weak material, only sets it in relief.

Matinee of Graham favorites and gee, the thrill of installing into the dusty present these old-time necessities and hoping JH would find them good, but also the attempts to squelch fuzzy disappointment running all through. Without Martha in this skin, that pose, how genial, how inevitable, really, is each of Jocasta's gyrations? And in a demi-dud like

Circe, where, finally, is craft. She fortunately's been canonized and deserves it more than, say, a Schweitzer, for she's a creator and (with Picasso and Auden and Stravinsky gone) the last giant on earth. Yet for anyone who can still come down from the clouds there's a lot of imperfection there.

The need to shake off accumulations of proud achievement no less than of debris. Yet free of the past we are inexistent: we die, really, of broken backs.

Gide's quip that France's greatest poet was *"Victor Hugo, hélas!"* came constantly to mind as one after another the new ballets trotted themselves out during the current "Hommage à Ravel." Choreographically Balanchine's company is the world's best, but it's not that good. True, there is no best anything; and Balanchine for a quarter-century has supplied enough invention to satisfy the most jaded minds and hearts. But the core has begun to soften, as happens with all absolute monarchies, and the softening is particularly evident in this festival. None of the seventeen new ballets will outlive the season. I declare this not with relish but with sadness.

Not that the creators were exhausted, but their choice of music was a mistake. Maybe Ravel cannot be danced to, not with any serious artistic result, not even *Daphnis et Chloé*, his only score composed *for* dance. The music seems at once too fragile and too complex for dance, too gorgeous, too self-contained. It doesn't impel movement as Stravinsky's muscularity does, nor do the movers urgently illuminate sounds. On the contrary, both music and dance seem diminished by their union.

This slant's biased. Knowing every note of every piece since prepubescence, I have built-in associations. Dangerous.

If you love something deeply, the instinct is both to share and to covet. Suddenly here's all this sound, once "mine," being manipulated in a manner that drains rather than swells.

Stronger the music, weaker the dance. *Daphnis et Chloé* and *L'Enfant et les sortilèges* have always defied choreography. They are the two most beautiful works of our century. The additions by John Taras and by Balanchine were lilies gilded.

Weaker the music, stronger the dance. Of the new Robbins ballets I liked best the first twenty seconds of the six-minute *Une barque sur l'océan* based on the composer's most amorphous number (and were those five males evoking waves, or people among waves?), and least *Chansons madécasses* based on the composer's most purposeful—indeed, his only "political"—music. Robbins avoided literary content and pasted pale decals onto bright substance. *Ma Mère L'Oye*, willfully rather than naturally childlike, patronized Ravel's most faultless diamonds. (Can one patronize diamonds?) As for *Introduction et Allegro*, if the program didn't state it was by Robbins, I'd have thought the dancers were in self-expression therapy making up the steps as they went along.

Indeed, this arbitrary yet literal translation of music—this letting the notes carry the dancer along (Mickeymousing rather than going against)—was a blight over all. *Pavane*, with chiffon scarf and mourning nymphet, evoked Isadora, who, like the cygnettes designed by D'Amboise, went in one eye and out the other.

Few scores composed expressly to be danced to have been first-rate; those that have have mostly outlived their choreography. Of the scores of scores commissioned by Martha

Graham only Copland's *Appalachian Spring* has survived on its own. The three greatest pieces commissioned by Diaghilev have *never* had great choreography (can they ever?): *Jeux, Sacre* and *Daphnis*—music which ridicules any dancemaster who approaches. On the other hand, some of the greatest ballets (and also works by modern dance giants) have been based on already existing music, or on made-to-order music by weaker composers. Really good music and really good choreography, when composed simultaneously by collaborators, seem to cancel each other out. The most famous exceptions are by Balanchine and Stravinsky (except for *Sacre*), and by Copland and Graham. (Naturally I'm concerned strictly with the twentieth century, not with ballets of, say, Rameau, Lully, Tchaikovsky.)

Television

Tom Wolfe on Buckley's program. Buckley comes off better than his guest. Political reactionaries who are also well-off educated Catholics often care—really romantically care—about the fact of art more than do hip non-Catholics. In any case, Wolfe should not place himself in a position of defending his slight essay, which should speak for him. His justification for facts becomes restatement of other facts: he was *there,* so he *knows* by what risible trickery such and such a Franz Kline was drummed up. Thus Wolfe churns the recipe for how Great Art must be made, and if an artist deviates he's not Great. As though all art were not largely a happy accident. Can even Wolfe, or for that matter the Renaissance painter himself, tell you why this crucifixion is finer than that, based on the same dimension and subject and commissioned by the same etc.?

As often in these discussions the essential is never mentioned, namely, that money—not esthetics—is the moving force in the art world (as opposed to the music or poem world) since paintings are commodities, investments (which poetry and music aren't).

Similarly in TV discussions of euthanasia we see a cultured paraplegic, monstrous physically, but lucid and defensive of her right to live, subjected to every sort of intimate question except how much money her parents have. Obviously, it's to the poor that we would grant the right to die.

Last night Channel 2 presented Walt Whitman to his homeland through a novel personification by W. C. Fields —I mean Rip Torn. A case could be argued (though I won't argue it) that no American theater is great because no American theater—unlike all other historic theater— deals with royalty. Our novels can be great because they can be poetical, fantastic, and don't need kings. Theater can never be successfully unrealistic. Whitman is no substitute for royalty, in any case.

Though she twitters more purely than a lark in Eden, one heart sinks as cameras pan in on "Woman of the Year," gracious Beverly Sills, mouthing smarmy nontruths. Only twenty years ago (she contends) our idea of culture was Europe, while today a soprano like herself stars at the Met, and she exhorts us to consider her a 100 percent American artist. Well, her repertory is 100 percent European, and at least 100 years old. And she's hardly the first American to hit the Met with a splash. A half-century ago Emma Eames, Farrar and Tibbett were singing there *in English*. What about Grace Moore, Louise Homer, Swarthout, Peters, Tucker and Peerce? Or Steber, Kirsten, Jepson, Thebom, Merrill, Dobbs and Price? Alone, black American singers were world-famous two generations back: Robeson, Hayes, Anderson, Maynor. And female recitalists in the forties— Tangeman, Fairbank, Neway, Howland, Curtin—did in an hour more for American music than Sills in her whole career. Let her continue to give out trippingly on the tongue, but enough of her false claims. For such claims are pernicious inasmuch as the arty rabble listens as to a sage and is thus exonerated from any responsibility.

8 · Song

What the world needs is a Society for the Promotion of Last Performances. In declaring a moratorium on The Hundred Masterpieces, the Society would reserve prizes for those artists who are the first to give the last hearings of Beethoven and Brahms. The prize money would go, of course, to new music. And since all living composers have a vested disinterest in standard programming they would prove useful in drawing up the rules.

Are composers really that bad off? Yes, some. American song composers are.

Vocal contours depend upon language and eventually give music a discernible national character. Vocal music is the source of non-vocal music, and speech inflection is the direct basis of all music of all cultures. So, since music resembles the speech of a nation, it also resembles the people. People therefore resemble their music.

In theory, the definitive interpreter of a country's songs should be a singer from that country.

In "Our Music Now" I point out that America is a land of specialists in everything but song literature while Europe produces general practitioners in everything but song literature.

Voice students in Germany, France and Italy logically master the songs of their own language first, often to the lifetime exclusion of all songs from other countries; the great foreign singers sing primarily in their native tongue. Americans, illogically, learn songs in foreign languages first (languages which they neither speak nor think in), often to the exclusion of American—or even English—works, whose existence they ignore; the most famous American singers sing primarily in foreign tongues.

Famous Americans in local recitals during the current season have sung mostly in German. (One or two may throw in some token Ives learned under duress last year because of that composer's big birthday.) They defend themselves. "Yes, but *my* Schumann is exemplary." "Would you sing him in Munich?" "I wouldn't dare."

Fischer-Dieskau, as the exceptional European general practitioner, is more prepared than most Americans for giving an all-English-language program tomorrow.

Recitals by opera stars? These are not recitals but bouquets of airs cut down to piano size. "I'd far rather do lieder," declares the American diva, "but my fans demand arias." Fans take what they're given. And divas, despite their protestations, sing what they believe in. Alas, since they also believe in fans, the circle turns vicious.

Evelyn Lear, biting hands that fed her, repeatedly states: "Thank God my coach forced me to give up modern stuff, it almost ruined my voice. Composers should take lessons if they want to learn to write grateful vocal music."

But Callas and Tebaldi ruined *their* voices on standard stuff. Meanwhile, that tiny handful of specialists—Beardslee, Curtin, Gramm, Wolff—sound better than ever after decades of doing contemporary music along with their "grateful" programs. That's because they don't treat modern music as modern music, but as music. No music of any period, if a singer believes in it, can harm the voice. (But aren't those broad jumps of Mozart and high dives of Bach riskier than anything Stravinsky ever penned?)

As for composers taking singing lessons, that would only reveal their own limitations rather than another's possibilities. Knowing how to sing has nothing to do with composing musically, hence vocally (for all true music, be it Paganini or Varèse, is in essence song). That composers have never been singers has obviously not kept them from creating the definition of vocality. When they follow a singer's suggestion (professional composers do listen) it's always to make a passage not simpler but harder.

"English is bad to sing in," say American singers. Because they comprehend the words they can no longer hear them, and are slightly embarrassed. Of course, the only bad thing about musicalized English is bad English. But our singers have been geared to language as medium, not message. Indeed, the only language any of us hears purely is the one we don't understand. When we learn to think in a new language we can no longer just listen to it because we know what it "means." Insofar as songs are literary they are not strictly music, and so (as Gertrude Stein says) they make us feel funny. Yet that funny feeling is exactly what all nonvocal music seeks to provide.

Sutherland is a dumb singer of dumb music. Sills is a smart singer of dumb music. Curtin is a smart singer of smart music. (Dumb singers of smart music? No example comes to mind, though there used to be "voiceless" singers of smart music.)

This is not to denigrate but to identify categories. I use dumb in the sense of *bête:* appealing to the body—as opposed to the intellect—through beat and tune, avoiding byways of harmonic density and contrapuntal nuance. Thus all rock and *bel canto* is dumb, while no serial dodecaphony is. The best of Poulenc—himself the best songwriter of this age—is dumb, and Stravinsky is dumber than he's given credit for (the early vocal ballets, *Noces* and *Histoire,* being pure carnality, as by extension are *The Rake's Progress* and *Requiem Canticles*). Bach is dumb in most of the well-tempered preludes and in the middle movements of his sonata structures, smart in fugues and choral pieces.

Dumbness which tries for smartness fails, like *The Rake's Progress.* Smartness which tries for dumbness fails, like Salzman's *Nude Paper Sermon.* The mixture of innocence and experience jells only when inadvertent, as sometimes in Satie or Scriabin.

Sills is intelligent about analyzing that which requires no analysis, but at least her diction and stage action are cleaner than Sutherland's. Curtin is more "important": she knows what she's up to in scores that ask that she know what she's up to.

Is Billie Holiday a dumb singer of dumb music? Yes, because what she does, and what she does it to, is uncomplicated and unliterary. Is Gerard Souzay a dumb singer of smart music? No, because, although his approach to all art is instinctive rather than scholarly, the contemporary music in which he specializes is of the nonintellectual brand, that is, French.

The French, curiously, who are nothing if not practical, have for three centuries produced a music whose attraction is essentially sensual. Germans, who are nothing if not emotional, are the ones who come up with the systems.

Awestruck by Mozart, people ask how he made magic from mere scales, and they cite the slow ebbing strings at the climax of *Don Giovanni*. Then they proffer their own non-answer: He was Mozart!

A real answer: Assuming the strings *are* magic, they are not "mere" scales. Mere scales are just that, mere, and get boring in lesser Mozart sonatas. However, in his opera the composer does turn a seven-note melodic minor mode into two (ascending, then descending) eight-note harmonic minor passages. He immediately repeats this pattern a half-tone higher, then a whole tone higher, and so on up chromatically, ever tightening the screw with this pseudomodulatory device (or vise) much copied in today's pop songs. Meanwhile a human basso intones a pedal "A" whose color alters according to the flux of color beneath, above, and beside it. These independent occurrences are melded by "abstract" chords of sustained lower brass, by a kettledrum heartbeat, and by the Commendatore's "concrete" language. Now, this concrete language—Italian prose—is missing from Mozart's first and only "plant" of the menacing mood, hours earlier, in the overture. But because the plant hints to connoisseurs what is to come (though the curtain's not yet up and human voices haven't yet been introduced), the scales in the overture may justly be termed psychological, a word inappropriate to any wholly nonvocal music, including Beethoven's quartets.

Mozart's "mere" scale was but one of many simultaneous happenings on his page: we may be aware of just that scale while the rest is subliminal, but that rest, while maybe magic, is analyzable magic.

That paragraph voices but one of many warnings about oversimplifying the gift to be simple. It's hard to be easy. Simplicity results from complex tailorings.

Is it time for black concertizers to desist from spirituals? Already years ago Leontyne Price sang hers unaccented (though her Barber and Harrison and even her Sauguet were edged in croon). Today Shirley Verrett, whose German and French are unaccented, fakes that drawl in her encores as white Helen Jepson used to do. Younger black singers learn the drawl from records.

Creatively considered, an ear for speech and an ear for music are never found together. Great composers don't write great verse, great poets don't compose great music. If a great songwriter—Schubert, say—does join through sound his ear for notes and verse, the verse is always by someone else. Often that someone is no one special. (Wagner, Menotti, Blitzstein, Noël Coward, who composed great music on their own words, are not often considered great poets.)

It is common practice for composers to shape fine music around preexisting words, but no poets have ever shaped fine verses around preexisting music, certainly not their own music. Even in pop, that casual yet profiteering domain, words generally come first.

The singing voice is the most satisfying of all instruments, the spoken voice is the least. Melodrama, or unmetered speech imposed upon music, like a gnat on a lens, intrudes on the business at hand. A composer may have conceived his music as coexistent with speech (*Le Martyre de Saint Sébastien, A Lincoln Portrait*), but the words always act as irritant.

Metered speech, with the declamation notated, as in Schoenberg's *Pierrot Lunaire* or Walton's *Façade*, is more satisfying, the voice part having been rhythmicized and hence controlled by the composer. This is song once removed. Even the fifties habit of reading poetry to jazz background, although inane, worked theatrically, since the musical improvisor was in cahoots with the actor.

A case could be made (but I shall not make it) that vocal music is deep or shallow according to its literal sense. Precise meaning is all-important to the enjoyment of melodrama or pop; indeed, the music often can't exist without the words. But no knowledge of Latin liturgy is needed to enjoy a mass of Palestrina; indeed, who can prove that Palestrina even "felt" the words, or that he did not impose these words upon tunes already in his notebook? (Isn't Handel's *Messiah*, that monument of inevitability, actually confected from preexisting scraps of profane operas?)

If you stop to think about it, there is something silly about singing poems. There is something silly about setting poems to music. There is even something silly about writing poetry. If you stop to think about it, what have you left?

Part Three

9. *Tennessee Now and Then*

By an early age most artists have stored up enough "life" to draw upon forever. Even the greatest have a finite number of themes which they vary throughout their careers. The variation is refinement, reexperienced experience, echo. Art manipulates echo by refashioning (or personalizing) works by another, or by oneself at another time. Still, there is a golden echo and a leaden echo, as one poet sang years ago, and as Tennessee Williams demonstrates today.

His style has always been personal despite proximity of excellent friends—"Southern" and otherwise. Yes, he does show a dash of the meanness, whimsy, blasé anger and pussycat anxiety of McCullers, Capote, Vidal and the Bowleses (Jane and Paul). He too blends sexuality with horror. But he has more fun than the others, and more ease with words.

His content too is his own. Or, to situate through analogy,

mix Jean Genet with Isaac Singer. Though Williams is as Goyish as Singer is Yiddish, both share an affection for (indeed, extract their identity from) what lies directly under hand, even when that is neither a bagel nor bourbon but a dybbuk's sigh or Martian spacecraft. They render the fantastic usual and the usual fantastic. . . . Though Williams is as American as Genet is French, both are drawn to the glamour of injustice, and both call forth a similar *dramatis personae:* tough guys, black giants, mad queens, policemen, angels.

But Williams' social spectrum is broader than theirs. Singer emits but one ethnic tonality, from Lublin to Broadway. Genet, in his stories, embraces neither women nor the rich. Now, Tennessee Williams' drawl is no less persuasive than his cosmopolitan repartee, his women are real (reread *The Vine* to quell that canard about men in drag), and his geographies are international. Also he has as good an ear as any author today.

He does not, as they say, have an ear for music (musically he is unperceptive, even deaf to all but the most naïve moods), but an ear for spoken situations. That ear, plus his contagious sense of the vastly carnal, has made him famous in the theater, where such qualities are showbiz effects as much as artistic virtues. When distilled in the fiction they bring forth an artist with no further need of a stage.

What makes him him? The large scope and mimetic gift. He is the ventriloquist of the underprivileged, rich and poor.

By 1965 Tennessee Williams' major themes had been mutually nourishing for twenty years. Big and little tales and plays ricocheted off each other, igniting always apparently novel combinations of energy, as a kaleidoscope confects endless patterns from limited colors. *The Yellow Bird* joined *The Glass Menagerie,* then shattered into *Summer and*

Smoke, which faded back into a little fable called "The Resemblance Between a Violin Case and a Coffin." Meanwhile one small story, "Three Players of a Summer Game," swelled into a large drama, *Cat on a Hot Tin Roof,* while another large drama, *The Milk Train Doesn't Stop Here Anymore* (starring reincarnations of the false poet from *Orpheus Descending* and the mad diva from *Sweet Bird of Youth*), was thrust back into a small story named "Man Bring This Up Road," only to reemerge as a play, again called *Milk Train,* which would receive still further polishing in a little prose piece, "The Inventory at Fontana Bella." The dead hustler of *One Arm,* reborn and heterosexualized as Stanley Kowalski, turned half-queer again in *Hard Candy,* became the character of Chicken in a story, "The Kingdom of Earth," took to the stage in *The Seven Descents of Myrtle,* where he married and lived content. The gorgeous rough trade, those likable whores, offensive grandes dames, despised versifiers, and fragile introverts were shuffled and renamed but remained intact and were treated with devotion. Fear of aging, need to travel, compassion for marriage, obsession with quickie sex, all this was perpetually intertwined with humane twists.

Little of the author's offspring from this period was without siblings or cousins, but the best of his only children live within the stories. Alone in his theater catalogue, like a white elephant with a cannon, stands the awkward *Camino Real,* which aims high at intellectual poesy but hits neither rhyme nor reason. Meanwhile among his twenty-odd short fictions—most of them diamonds—glimmer unidentifiable gems shaped like hearts: surely "Desire and the Black Masseur," "Mysteries of the Joy Rio," and "Mama's Old Stucco House" are the rarest love stories in English. All are set in gold.

It comes as no surprise that the six tales in Williams' brief new book—his first collection in eight years—should prove to be reconsiderations of their writer's younger triumphs. The ricochet has boomeranged, self-nourishment is now self-cannibalism, the echo lacks resonance and falls like lead. The *Eight Mortal Ladies Possessed* are caricatures, all more or less unpleasant, of Tennessee's gold stars.

The first and best of the vignettes, "Happy August the Tenth," describes simply the cohabitation of two modern bourgeois women whose rapport is equivocal (do they or don't they?), who call each other by last names (Horne and Elphinstone), and who quarrel and perhaps don't make up. It rings as almost true as its precursor, the short and sad play called *Something Unspoken* about a pair of old-fashioned aristocrat females who quarrel and do make up. Like the play, the story is mostly duologue (but could be dramatized only to its detriment) and Williams continues with the clean French rule of omitting quotation marks around speech. Also featured is the less-happy mannerism of inserting pronouns before proper nouns as solution to the problem all authors find when writing about several people of one sex. ("... and she, Horne, had shrieked at her ... but she, Horne, had reminded Elphinstone that she had her mother's cool retreat ... while she, Horne, had to adhere to a rather strict schedule.") Here too is a writer willing to belittle the very psychoanalysis which in "real life" he has publicly declared to be a tormenting salvation. And we learn a new word: *lallocropia*, defined by Elphinstone as the psychiatric term for a compulsion to use shocking language.

"The Inventory at Fontana Bella" turns out to be an unfunny sequel to the never very funny *Milk Train*. Disagreeable Mrs. Goforth is revived as a centenarian principessa with all the dignity of a Mr. Magoo in Antonioniville. There is nothing literarily wrong in depicting a stupid, greedy, senile bitch who dreams of "the ecstasy of penetration." Yet this one, herself representative of nothing, is garbed in sophomoric symbolism ("All good morticians have telephone numbers consisting of nothing but zero, zero, *ad infinitum*"). Her foulmouthing, once grandly obscene, has grown trivially vulgar, her inventor himself not being immune to lallocropia.

"Miss Coynte of Greene" floats to us through the extinguished embers of *Summer and Smoke*. In the earlier work the radical about-face of Alma (like that of Thaïs or of Sadie Thompson) is counterpointed by a reverse action in the hero, and the moral is that there is no moral: bad turns good while good turns bad. Now Miss Coynte's "emancipation" evolves from nothing and so contrasts with nothing, with the moral that nymphomania, in itself, leads to fulfillment and thence to blissful death. Years ago the same spermy moral spouted baroquely from *The Kingdom of Earth*; today it falls with a rococo ring. Years ago, because they were spoken from the stage, the author got away with lines such as "The sky looks like a great white bone"; today on the page, without benefit of vocal timbre, the corn is less sweet: "From birth we go so easily to death, it is really no problem unless we make it one for us." Years ago Williams' habit of throwing asides to the reader seemed quaintly purposeful as in "Two on a Party" (". . . his sybaritic existence which suited him better than the dubious glory of being a somewhat better than hack writer of Hollywood film scenarios and so forth. Yes, and so forth!"); today the habit seems coyly purposeless when, in the middle of a paragraph he tells us that he, the author, is now going into the next room to watch Walter Cronkite, and before he goes he will type three asterisks in a row, which the editor may remove if he chooses.

The heroine of "Sabbatha and Solitude" takes after She of *Sweet Bird of Youth*. While the horny drunk tantrums of Princess Kosmonopolis were credible because she was no heavy thinker but a fallen star, it's hard to swallow the horny drunk tantrums of Miss Veyne Duff-Collick, world-renowned contriver of sonnet sequences: Isadora Duncan dancing Marianne Moore. Not bad as farce, which, alas, this is not. Once in an elegy called "The Poet" Tennessee foresaw with pathos the ordeal by which someone like Allen Ginsberg might gain glory with the young. Here he takes a mean swipe at the real Ginsberg as derider of the past—as someone who literally usurps the heat of his deranged poetess.

Better is the fifth story, "Completed," which starts: "Although Miss Rosemary McCool was approaching the age of twenty she had yet to experience her first menstruation." Rosemary's put-upon mother obliges the poor misfit to attend a small private school named Mary, Help a Christian, and later to attend her own coming-out party which is climaxed by hate and hysterics, and with the malady of menstruation. The malady draws the young woman to a demented but sympathetic aunt in the shadow of whose solidarity she will remain forevermore. Williams can still exhume unusual youth-age conditions so lively with excruciation that we wince. Yet the pity of *The Glass Menagerie* has gone up in cold smoke.

The last and least of the stories, composed in 1944 (predating the others by some twenty-nine years), is a mood piece entitled "The Red Part of a Flag or Oriflamme." It deals vaguely with a girl who—she too—protests her coming of age through fantasy, and who, on buying a red silk dress which she *dares* to don in daylight, provokes in her inventor such outpourings as: "It flashed, it flashed. It billowed against her fingers. Her body surged forward. A capital ship with cannon. Boom. On the far horizon. Boom. White smoke is holy. Nobody understands it. It goes on, on, without the world's . . ." Why go on? The story resembles Williams' verse, which is honest perhaps (that is, not prose, not doggerel), but diluted, harmless. Strong poetry burns. This patter doesn't singe a hair.

Clearly the author believes in these stories both as art and as message, and possibly as a "breakthrough" in style. His belief is his privilege—nor dare one find fault with new language. But this is not even new grammar, merely new accents—terrifically up-to-date—that inelegantly blur the line between grandiloquence and satire.

Some artists develop and change, if not always in quality, at least in scope: Beethoven and Picasso, for instance, had "periods." Others emerge full-blown from Zeus's head; they don't advance, but neither do they regress: Henry James and Ravel, as proficient at the beginning as at the end of their lives, continually manufactured the same *kind* of product—nor can we always tell early from late models. Still others bloom with late models: had Elliott Carter, say, or Erick Hawkins died twenty years ago they might be unknown today, their singularity having lain dormant until middle years.

Another breed of artist burns himself out alive, lives on as a shell, yet who can say? Rimbaud renounced it all, but had he survived another decade could he have slipped back into genius? Today would the very denial of his art be named genius? If a composer like Samuel Barber or a painter like Larry Rivers seem spent, wait! they can reexplode tomorrow. Solon was surely not the first to point out twenty-five hundred years ago that no man can be called washed up until he dies. The quiescent Verdi composed a masterpiece at eighty, the very age that Strauss made a glittering comeback. And how about Monet? Or Ruby Keeler?

Nonetheless, American playwrights, big and little, fall without repeal into that pigeonhole of the prematurely sterile. None, not Miller or Inge or Albee, not Hellman or Laurents or Anderson, have in the past years come up with anything worthy of their younger efforts. Tennessee Williams is no exception. His plays produced since 1960 are similar but inferior to those produced before.

American theater has little to do with mature philosophic analysis and much to do with the pure energy one finds in animals or children. When our dramatists try Think Pieces they give us either artifacts like *Tiny Alice* or propaganda like *The Crucible*. They never spark the theological fireworks of a Mauriac, a Montherlant, a Cocteau, a Claudel, even a Sartre; our public doesn't care about morality issues beyond pop melodramas like *The Exorcist*. We aren't raised that way. Neither are our dramatists, who, after all, form a part of their own audience. (In France, conversely, there exists no wholly lay audience.) Thus a mature vitality has not yet been directed toward our theater.

Of all the exhausted dramatists in America still at the game, Tennessee is the only one with a trump card: his ability to write straight fiction. The new stories are so fragile that when absorbed into their creator's *oeuvre* they won't disturb the surface, nor will they pollute the depths as do the later plays. They scarcely smell of those gas leaks of compromise that seep into even his best drama and permeate the worst, like that recent corny Saroyanesque foray called *Small Craft Warnings*. (His titles do remain wonderful.)

In a notorious essay twenty-seven years ago Mary Mc-
Carthy "accused" Tennessee Williams of being a success. To
succeed meant to sell out by studding one's work with
enough variety for the whole family. Shakespeare too was
guilty of such variety. McCarthy was right; her own career
has since proved that success need not be a dirty word, for
like Williams she has stood the test of time.

Still, no short-story writer can live off his stories, but must
supplement his income with professorships, film scenarios,
talk shows. Exceptionally, Tennessee need no longer resort
to these outlets. As another Williams was a poet who lived
as a doctor, so Tennessee Williams is a storyteller who lives
as a dramatist; his late plays are leaden, but surely the early
ones bring in enough silver to permit him to focus more on
the mining of his fiction talent and to bring up the gold
that will balance the scales.

10·Nabokov's Bagázh

My gaudiest musical memory is from 1952 in Paris—that least musical of cities—when for thirty April nights a festival called "Masterpieces of the Twentieth Century" offered mixed pleasures to an international elite. One after another major revivals and massive premieres, by Stravinsky, Thomson, Berg, Britten, and scores of others, were conducted by Monteux, Markevich, or the composers themselves, all immaculately produced, and very, very costly. The funds came from the CIA, a fact then not known to the diasporic Jack-of-all-artistic-trades who single-handedly launched the evenings, Nicolas Nabokov.

Nicolas Nabokov has never been a public name so much as a force behind public names. He has known everyone worth knowing in the world of music, and they have all known him. If, during the fifty years that he has engaged in unremunerative pursuits to benefit fellow artists, he has been less flamboyant than a Hurok, that is because he is more concerned with creators than with performers—more concerned with What than with How.

Promoting the What, Nabokov, after the Paris success, organized similar festivals in other world capitals. He has also been a professor (notably at St. John's College, where he overhauled the Great Books curriculum), U.S. Cultural Adviser in Berlin, political activist (he co-founded with Mary McCarthy the Red-baiting "American Intellectuals for Freedom" in 1949), commentator for *Voice of America*, editor of a series of books on modern music, and a theater director and producer. Distinct from these various occupations, the man Nabokov has been continually a composer. His catalogue is understandably short, but over the years since his 1928 ballet *Ode* for Diaghilev, the output has been serious and solid, with two full-scale operas, *Rasputin's End*, to a libretto by Spender, and *Love's Labour's Lost*, libretto by Auden.

Nicolas Nabokov is also an author. Twenty-five years ago he published *Old Friends and New Music*, and now on the same subject but in the form of memoirs comes a second book—despite the protest that he does not pretend to be a writer. Maybe the protest is a red herring, for to read the opening of *Bagázh* (Russian for baggage, peripatetic) is vaguely to reread the memoirs of Nicolas' famous cousin, the one who collects butterflies. Routines of those well-off cultured infants during the *ancien régime* were not unalike, and the intent of both was to evoke such routines solely through a trust in memory's capacity for truth. But for the musician the debris of dreams floats in less fragrant amber than for the novelist. *Bagázh* is well under way before sounds of music are heard, and only then does it take off on its own. For if Cousin Vladimir was not drawn to music (in-

deed, like so many great writers he was—is—unembar-
rassedly ignorant, even contemptuous of the art), for Nicolas music defined living, and hence his character.

His character emerged with the revolution when the
Nabokov clan established itself in Berlin. Most Russian ex-
patriates—Stravinsky, for instance, or Tchelitchew—were
of Gallic inclination, but Nicolas' long German sojourn
irrevocably stamped both his music and personality. It was
there he began to hear concerts, mostly in attendance with
an uncle who informally but finally was his most vital in-
structor. He became a reviewer for a Russian-language daily
("The only way to deal with a piece of music is to listen to
it well and then bombard it with the best words one can
find"), and began to have his own pieces performed. Pros-
pects of other performances, or sometimes the mere need for
proximity to other musicians, led him to France, and finally
to the United States. Candidly he discusses connections,
even affections, but his income sources remain hazy, and
never a word about his health, his romantic life (though he
is much married), nor the romantic life of others. For this
is what he calls "a book about friendship," and so it is.

About the content and shape of new music in general and
the economics that surround it, Nabokov is clear-minded
and farseeing. About his own music he is reticent. One short
paragraph suffices for personal esthetic, which is that he has
no esthetic beyond being tonal, nonexperimental, consistently tuneful, belonging unmindfully to his generation,
and composing what "sounds Russian to foreign ears." However, the texture of Nabokov's briefly expressed concerns as
a composer will come as news to lay readers who "love
music." He does not extol the thrill of creativity; rather he
underlines the horror of amateurism, of half-empty halls, of
some crooked managers, in short, revealing the vulnerability

(instead of the smugness) deep-seated in all true artists. Nor does he talk much about performers. If an occasional vocalist is referred to, it is never by name.

Elsewhere names fly thick and fast. Maritain, Gershwin, Cocteau, Prokofiev, all are claimed as staunch acquaintances but never heard from again, while legends whom the author met but once and scarcely knew are recalled at length. Long pages devoted to the dilapidated Isadora tell only what we've heard a hundred times. Long pages devoted to the ailing Rilke relate only what the musician told the poet (how Lenin's upper-class accent contradicted what he said), not what the poet replied. Maybe Rilke wasn't talking.

Indeed, if one thing is frequently confirmed here, it is that great artists save their greatness for their art and don't squander it in conversations, even with each other. Lesser lights sometimes shine brighter—the grandmothers, for example. One, the traditional regal iceberg in black, admonishes Nicolas for six pages: "Never stick your *pipiska* into a girl"; the other sums up a lost epoch when she chides her older son for flirting with his younger brother: "What are the servants for?" And there are grand portraits of bigger fish: Of his harmony teacher, the obese and original Rebikov, who froze to death at the end of the revolution, and whose unpublicized influence on Debussy possibly changed the flow of French music. Of Diaghilev who, far more than a *régisseur*, was a wet nurse and matchmaker and always in debt. Of Stravinsky, whose social *moeurs* and compositional processes he analyzes much more deeply than his own. Of Harry Kessler, a German Charlus; of Pyotr Abrassimov, an enigmatic ambassador; and especially of Auden, whose dying days, though powerfully fructuous, seemed lonesome and cranky and filled with longings to end it all.

Nicolas Nabokov himself is never cranky, except about

Soviet Russia. The political state provokes a nagging contempt, the country a physical loathing. Thus one would
have welcomed more reaction to his chosen homeland,
America—accounts, say, of the noted American composers
known to be his friends. For he has done as much as any
Russian since Koussevitzky toward putting American music
on the map.

11 · *Britten's* Venice

For two centuries after the death of Henry Purcell in 1695, England produced no music of consequence. With Benjamin Britten's birth in 1913 the land awoke like Sleeping Beauty and picked up where she had left off. As though reincarnated, Purcell himself was Britten's main influence and love.

Britten in turn is the main influence, if not love, of English musicians today. Like a huge magnetic tuning fork his conservatism sets their tone: some resist, but by that resistance acknowledge the tone which they cannot shut out long enough to move toward other fields of attraction. In a sense, Britten even influenced his immediate predecessors (Vaughan Williams, Berkeley, Tippett, Holst, Walton, Bax, forever awash in the so-called modes of Hellenism and of Renaissance Albion) since he bettered them at their game and they knew it.

He is the utter eclectic. Not conventional so much as traditional, he does not fall back on the set grammar but pulls it up into his special syntax. It would be difficult to find in Britten's catalogue any measure not somehow attributable to another composer, yet each measure is somehow stamped with his technical trademarks just as each overall work is redolent of his human fixations.

His trademarks are metaphors. Like all artists, Britten does the undoable. In giving nonvocal music a recognizable meaning beyond its "abstract" meaning he becomes, more literally than Debussy ever dreamt of being, an impressionist, a metaphorist rather than a similist. This he manages through orchestrational tours de force and through obsessional rhythmic patterns. (In his new opera, for example, his brushed drums *are* what you hear—not *like* what you hear—from vaporetto motors; his dipping viola patterns *are* what you hear from dripping gondola paddles.) His vocal music too is metaphoric. He treats speech values more eccentrically, investing them with the personal pulse of tension and release, convincingly filling the empty areas of pure music with the impurities of literature.

His human fixations are chiefly aquaphilic and pedophilic. Not only is water more than mere decor in operas like *Peter Grimes, Billy Budd* and *Albert Herring,* but a case could be made for the warm melancholy of water submerging his nontheater vocal works as well, like the songs in *Nocturne, Lacrymae,* and *On This Island.* Young boys are the *raison d'être* of such operas as *Peter Grimes, Billy Budd* and *The Turn of the Screw;* they cast a central glow from some chamber and choral works (*Canticle 2, Saint Nicholas,* the *Michelangelo Sonnets*) and, by Freudian extension, from some strictly instrumental pieces too, like the *Young Person's Guide to the Orchestra.* Britten has never set a drama on urban ground, nor on a theme of romantic love between man and woman.

For an eclectic rather than an innovator to dominate a country's art is fruitless: his followers in aping mere manner lack the verve of outright thieves. England's youngish explorers, such as Birtwistle and Davies, seem not to possess the force of true discovery and so have remained in the shade of the old.

Suddenly the shade starts to shimmer with new slants. Music's recent global style of willful opaqueness is clearing away. A modernistic brand of ugliness that everyone hated without admitting it is no longer being manufactured with the hope of being unpopular. The pendulum swings back to the right. Since Britain, thanks to Britten, always *was* right, British conservatism ironically is becoming the current avant-garde, and is represented by the "representational" scores of Bennett and Maw, who are in no way revolutionary or even resistant. They sprang full-blown and affectionate from the head of their foster parent, Sleeping Beauty. That parent meanwhile continues producing children of its own.

Benjamin Britten's musical language, cold for some, for me has always seemed warm and contagious, open to every dialect of mind and soul. But I was miffed, at first, by Britten's latest work, *Death in Venice*.

In preparation for the dress rehearsal I dutifully pondered the vocal score and couldn't make much of it. It did stress the trademarks and fixations—sea, youth, "forbidden" love —more candidly than ever, the metaphors turning psychoanalytically, if not musically, verbose as though the composer were forcing his dead collaborator's Germanisms onto his own native restraint. But the aftermath, at least on paper, looked sterile, padded, colorless, simplistic and, yes, lazy, with endless recitative on neumelike signs speckling an over-extended text. However, since this was a reduced blueprint (even Britten's full scores don't readily yield their secrets in print) by a musical dramatist who was nothing if not experienced, probably there was method in his drabness.

Sure enough, at the rehearsal the hall brimmed with noises of skill and beauty. What for the eye was a skeleton became for the ear—when fleshed out by an orchestra—a wealth of *trouvailles* which unexpectedly shined up the dusty narrative.

Since then, I've returned often to both live performance and to the score, and realized I'd originally missed some basic points (a reader's speed is never precise). Each verbal phrase, regenerated through live performance, exemplifies and redefines Britten's claim as the world's supreme melodist. If that claim was not immediately obvious in *Death in Venice* it was because the tunes were honed to microcosms. Those recitatives weren't recitatives at all, but total melodies refined to lowest terms. The elaborate book, filled with logical contradictions, could thus be imparted without sounding silly. If this music never "opens up" in the usual sense, it does so in reverse, like explosions in some galaxy seen through a microscope.

Melodists are those who flow rather than build, who let happen rather than make happen, who write tunes rather than figures—arched lines that feel singable rather than playable, lines that sound "sung" whether planned for human voice or for mechanical instruments. Melody is the surf in which Puccini bathed, as did Ravel and even Hindemith, breathing passively, propelled by nature more than by calculation.

Fragmentists whittle more artificial, more *complex* pieces, since fragments, like cells, innately lend themselves to re-arrangement and self-renewal.

Thus Chopin, who never composed for singers, was a melodist; Beethoven was not. Mahler, primarily an orchestral composer, was a melodist; Debussy, so happy with voices, was not. Thus Webern too was a melodist, not because his pieces aren't compact like Beethoven's (they are), but because his material is not reworked and developed.

(Which, finally, is more economical, the melodist or the fragmentist? A motive is a perennial which reblossoms in endless shapes, a piece of glass in a kaleidoscope. A melody can be heard a single time, spacious and inevitable, before, like a Cereus, it dies.)

Benjamin Britten is the only living composer equally skilled at melody and fragment, whether writing opera, small songs, or "pure" instrumental works of every shape. He merges these assets in combination.

Like Mozart, Britten has a knack for making mere scales more than mere. Consider the questioning dream before the phantasmagoria in Act Two, wherein four E-major modes set forth diatonically from low pitches, separate and float at different speeds to four unstable branches, alight, turn to solid silver and glitter fixedly, a frozen harmony derived from liquid counterpoints, a static plate upon which a roaming soliloquy is now etched. Again the modes ascend, and still again, each time climbing higher on the same common tones, each time arresting to form frames for the nervous words.

This simultaneity—this doing of more than one version of the same thing at the same time (literally the same thing, not variations, like a canon at the unison unfocused from too-closely-staggered entrances)—is Britten's metaphor at its most eloquent. Listen again to the scene in San Marco where the identical litany is chanted at two tempos, evoking not only the cathedral's echoing walls but a different (though simultaneous) viewpoint, or soundpoint, in the minds of Aschenbach and Tadzio. With traditionalists newness plays no part; novelty lies in perception more than in what is perceived. In *Death in Venice* Thomas Mann (also a traditionalist, carrying on rather than breaking through, so that, like Britten, he seemed to predate certain of his elders) did not tell what had never been seen, but what had always been seen and not noticed. In his opera, Britten, by telling what we've always heard without listening, revirginates our ears. Such perception is a thrilling and dangerous gift, a gift which both the novelist and the composer "lend" to their respective visions of Aschenbach, and which kills him.

The transfer of Thomas Mann's self-contained and well-known story into another medium could have been, at the very least, superfluous. Britten almost turns the trick because he has *framed* the text. Retaining intact the famous words, he has focused private colors on them from all around, and transported the finished tableaux for us to see and hear upon a stage. What we experience is a kind of masterpiece, although I'm not sure why, beyond the fact that it was composed with a marvelous ear for taste and tension. Nonetheless, two extraneous elements help to explain the specialness:

First is the well-timed collaboration of a dead and a living artist. Although Thomas Mann, whose hundredth birthday will soon be celebrated, was the first novelist to write with sensible intelligence (as opposed to emotional intelligence—for there was Proust, after all) about the musical creative process, none of his contemporaries ever set his fictions to music. Although ostensibly about the pull between a creator's sacred duties and profane desires or, as Mann put it, between Apollo and Dionysius, the subject is the waning of productivity as symbolized by the "mystery" of pederasty. Britten is the only composer ever to depict that matter centrally in opera. The matter needs his British understatement, not because homosexuality is the bizarre vice it seemed in 1912, but because today it is so very normal. We go along with myths like *Tristan* or *Turandot*, but stigmas of the not-too-distant past remain ticklishly close to our nominal magnanimity. Who any longer, when so openly all is said and sung, could possibly utter, and get away with it, the words of an old man suffering from a love that dare not speak its name?

Which brings up the second extraneous element: Peter Pears, the English tenor and Britten's lifelong friend, in the role of Aschenbach. Pears, who has realized most of the composer's vocal works in Europe, is now, at sixty-five, making his Metropolitan Opera debut. For one hundred and forty minutes he does not leave our view or our attention span. What some call his lack of opulence paradoxically lends his nonvoice a dimension of expressivity unknown to more standard tenors. His sentences are intoned with enviable clarity as though invented on the spot. For Pears is a thread of the score's very fabric: he appears to belong to the composer's living concept, and to the dead author's too, so serious and touching is his portrayal. To imagine another in the role is to imagine a harpsichord piece played on an organ.

Myfanwy Piper's adaptation is faithful to a fault. She includes in the libretto nothing not in the novella, down to the last subnotion and symbolic echo. With transposition from art to art, certain weights, while keeping balance, switch emphasis. A strawberry vendor, ominously recurrent in the story, becomes on stage an airy *refraineuse* risking comparison to another in *Porgy and Bess*.

Riskier still is Tadzio's realization. To make flesh of the ineffable is always a miscalculation. The success of parables like *Parsifal* or *Suddenly Last Summer*, or of characterizations like Kafka's petty-bourgeois K or Auden's great poet Mittenhoffer, lies in the invisible ideal. Tadzio inhabits our fantasy no less than Aschenbach's. To find him now in person, a *dancer*, is to find a perfectionist intent on selling his craft. Observed as a ballet sans text (which the opera is for anyone ignorant of English), *Death in Venice* becomes the saga of a flirty boy who lusts for an old man but whose mother interferes so he drowns himself.

If the Silent Ideal must be depicted within a medium whose very purpose is noise, then mime, while a bit illegal, is probably the only solution; indeed, Britten has effectively based at least one previous opera around a mute but visible child. But actually to choreograph vast portions of the piece, as Frederick Ashton was hired to do, in the set-number style of Rameau is deadening for a modern mood piece; and when the Silent Ideal is rendered as a champion athlete the careful craft of Thomas Mann, without a word changed, is utterly violated. Mann's Tadzio is no winner, but the passive recipient of everyone's love earned not through excellence but through innocence and beauty.

12 · Ezra Pound as Musician

Nothing is more bemusing than to discover in reappraisal that certain opinions once voiced by the truly great now appear quite naïve. The discovery is bemusing (rather than exasperating) because it invariably occurs in areas outside the Great Man's "specialty." (Had he been naïve *within* that specialty he would not, by definition, have been great.)

Specialists are what artists (also scientists and candlestick makers) of our century mostly become; if they develop an affection for one of the sister arts they fall prey to the same failings as any amateur: the confounding of acquaintance with knowledge, of conviction with greatness, effort with ability. One thinks of Claudel's or Henry James's verbalizations on painting—or this very remark on James and Claudel! When the concern is music, which it is here, a practicing musician merely smiles patiently as, say, André Gide tells him what Chopin is all about, or as E. M. Forster

—even Shaw—explains the art through poetic rather than analytic description. Composers, of course, class performers as laymen and consider men like Rubinstein or Casadesus as more sensical when playing than when writing, or writing about, music. Perhaps in a pinch a philosopher such as Susanne Langer can be attended precisely because she exorcises the phony inspirational Hollywoodiana from musical art.

Some poets are original and instructive when they discuss peripheral (i.e., theatrical) usages of music, sometimes even when they make librettos for their composer friends. But when venturing suggestions as to how their verse should be musicalized, or how the music itself should be built, they tread risky water—the very water in which Ezra Pound nearly drowned.

Nearly, but not quite. Between the two is continuing life. And life, with all that implies of curiosity and scholarly enthusiasm, is what, in the 1920s, the poet had in abundance.

Music reportage is more appropriate for performance than for composition, for how the execution occurred than what was executed, for what McLuhan calls (I think) the "hot medium" than what stays put. Berenson wrote real literature about paintings of the past because those paintings are stationary (hence, paradoxically, continual): they can be *referred to*. But Shaw's criticism of nineteenth-century musical execution becomes (since the performance is gone forever) less literature than history. There exists today a whole new style of recording criticism, and records, like pictures, stay put. But since, as the saying goes, God didn't intend music to be heard on discs, such art is makeshift. (Occasional music *is* designed to be heard only on recording, although nothing could be more self-contradictory than, for example, a record of "chance" music—and several exist.)

As to the instructive virtue of musical criticism, it tells the public who wasn't there what happened last night, or the public who *was* there what to *think* about what happened last night. To composers it will teach nothing about the quality or construction of pieces (score reading teaches that), but will maybe teach them something about how pieces can be played—including their own.

The music commentator, then, falls roughly into either of two classifications: 1) that of reporter on what just happened (press reviewer of concerts) or on what is happening (taste-maker); 2) that of reporter on what once happened (historian, biographer) or on what was happening (authors on the evolution of harmony out of plainchant and counterpoint).

Pound, by self-ordainment, becomes classified under each of these categories, though by what authority it is hard to say, for no one seems to know much about his formal musical training. He has, I'm told, passed much of his adult life in near contact with the once-successful violinist Olga Rudge; and during the twenties in France he hobnobbed (as did all literati) with various creative musicians, mostly American. One still suspects that his auditory education was come by less through discussion with these persons than through rigorous study of the prosodic values of Provençal, a language—like all others before the fifteenth century—quite intertwined with music. Certainly Pound's intellectual knowledge about music far surpassed his practical knowledge; his main concern (at least before meeting Antheil) seemed to have been between words, word rhythms and music. "Poetry atrophies when it gets too far from music, music when it gets too far from the dance" (*ABC of Learning*). And certainly also, emotional references to music are everywhere apparent in his verse, from *A Lume Spento* of 1908 to his 1956 translation of Sophocles' *Women of Trachis*. And names of musicians are scattered throughout the *Cantos*.

On this *propos* let me cite the very talented young triple-threat musician, my friend Robert Hughes, who in 1958 visited Pound at St. Elizabeth's and wrote me later as follows:

> I went down from Buffalo as part of a recorder quartet led by Forrest Read, a Pound scholar who has published on the *Cantos* (Columbia University Press, if I remember correctly). We played Gabrieli Canzone out on the lawn for Pound and his wife, and Pound said it was only the second time he had heard live music during his incarceration there—the first time having been a pianist brought by Stokowski. In addition to the soprano recorder I had my bassoon along, and having read that Pound at one time had played the instrument I offered it to him. He declined saying that he gave it up in the 20s in order to take up boxing with Hemingway. I asked him about *Le Testament* and he said that as a consequence of the war he had no idea where the manuscript or a copy could be found. He did, however, say that he had a page or two of his unfinished opera *Cavalcanti* and promptly fetched it from his room. It looked like a Ruggles manuscript—very large notes scribbled on broad wrapping paper. We played it for him: a simple troubadour-type tune, not terribly distinguished as a melody, but with a certain grace and ease for the voice.

Le Testament? A lost manuscript? An unfinished opera? Indeed yes! From his special knowledge Pound had, in the twenties, composed an opera. Whatever that opera's ultimate worth, is there another poet of the past two centuries who can claim as much?

The text was drawn from Villon's *Grand Testament* (1461), a number of funereal bequests in whimsically argotic yet highly poignant medieval forms of versification. The resulting libretto (or should it be termed rather a *chant-fable?*) amounts to an intoned "autobiography" of François Villon, in one act of around forty minutes. The musical score itself is certainly the work of a nonprofessional, e.g., much more finicky for the eye than it needs be for translation by the ear. Although George Antheil helped both in the exegesis and in the actual notation, the result remains that of an amateur: measures shifting from an unreasonably complex ⅝ to ¹³⁄₁₆ to etcetera could easily be simplified and still provide the smooth modal vocality intended by the poet. Nevertheless a self-justifying foreword to the manuscript deserves a quotation:

> This opera is made out of an entirely new musical technic, a technic, for certain, made of sheer music which upholds its line through inevitable rhythmic locks and new grips ... a technic heretofore unknown, owing to the stupidity of the formal musical architects still busy with organizing square bricks in wornout ... patterns ... a powerful technic that grips musical phrases like the mouths of great poets grip words.
>
> There is really nothing more to say. Those *who want to understand*, will understand Villon.
>
> As the opera is written in such a manner so that nothing at all is left to the singer, the editor would be obliged if the singer would not let the least bit of temperament affect in the least the correct singing of

this opera, which is written as it sounds! Please do not embarrass us by suddenly developing intelligence.

Paris thus heard it in 1926, and Virgil Thomson, who was there, declared "the music was not quite a musician's music, though it may well be the finest poet's music since Thomas Campion . . . and its sound has remained in my memory." The foreword's insecure insolence notwithstanding, the opera is of genuine and hauntingly unclassifiable beauty.

The beauty, though, was of such impractical difficulty that it was not until 1962 that the opera received a second hearing in a version made for the BBC by the Canadian composer Murray Schafer. Such is the material of the music that, like Mussorgsky, who is submitted to much rearrangement (or, more properly, like the *Art of the Fugue*), *Testament* "speaks" as well in various instrumentations. The Paris version was apparently for only two human voices, solo violin (Olga Rudge) and a *corne*, which is a twelve-foot instrument from medieval France. Schafer's bilingual rendition is a good deal more sophisticated, using full chorus, several soloists, and a complex of instruments including saxophone, mandolin, and rattled bones.

A few summers ago Gian-Carlo Menotti induced the poet from his Rapallo seclusion to attend another performance (only the third! and the first one ever staged) of *Testament* at the Spoleto Festival. In preparation for this event Menotti engaged two protégés, the bright composers Lee Hoiby and Stanley Hollingsworth, to revamp the work, shortening it and standardizing the notation. The result was then choreographed by John Butler, and offered to an elite international public whose reception was apparently one of high respect, puzzled indignation, and a standing ovation. The ovation was as much for Pound the poet as for Pound the composer. As for Pound the man, his presence at the spectacle is said to have been noncommittal, even dazed, and his brief spoken preamble was preceded by an untheatrically long silence.

Silence has come to be the tone of Ezra Pound today. I, for one, as a composer thinking of a poet, find the fact unutterably touching and telling—the silence in music, and in poetry, of one who once spoke perhaps not wisely but too well.

Robert Hughes said Pound thought little now about his music of the past, that it was remote, like all our pasts, like dreams, and that he is, silently, completing his life of Cantos.

This then—a career as composer of a single opera performed but thrice over a forty-year interval—represents Pound's qualification as music commentator. A qualification *after the fact*—for his book, which is the object of this discussion, was begun as early as 1918 and published a year before the first presentation of the opera.

The title is *Antheil and the Treatise on Harmony with Supplementary Notes by Ezra Pound*. It is divided into four sections of unequal length: "The Treatise on Harmony," "Antheil," "William Atheling," and "Varia."

The style, unlike the author's music, is pontifical, tries for wit, sometimes achieves rapidity and wisdom, more often ponderousness. A cultured lay genius like Pound can insist on learning the hard way (i.e., on his own) what a professional is simply taught at school and takes for granted. The lay genius will present the professional with his "unique" discoveries, while the professional, dull though he be, heaves a sigh for the genius, for the genius could have saved so much time by merely opening a book.

Pound gives us emotional talk on practical subjects, practical talk on esthetics. One quickly senses that he, at least below the surface, may feel less on home ground here as he speaks (so to speak) from outside in, than in, for instance, *ABC of Reading,* his other scholarly treatise, where he really speaks from inside out. Though *treatise* this present work is not—which is precisely what saves it—it contains none of the documentary orderliness of the usual doctorate. The effect is rather one of obsessions fragmented into a manner both folksy and grand, occasionally incomprehensible, not unlike the utterances of Ives or even, curiously, John Cage's *Diary.*

Antheil, who provides the impetus for the major portion of the volume, appears (despite Pound's obstinate veneration of him) to provide an excuse onto which the writer latches his theories—or rather his conclusions. By far the chief reason, in the cold of our time, to allow the hot air of these conclusions to flow interestingly over us, is because of the man, now almost historical and certainly silent, who once so feverishly committed them to paper.

Part One, *The Treatise on Harmony,* starts right off with an unfair question (though who expects poets to be fair?):

"What, *mon élève,* is the element grossly omitted from all treatises on Harmony . . ."

Does the *élève* now stare blankly because he must assume there's just one reply to this arbitrary query (a reply, what's more, unavailably cached within the questioner's smugness)?

Supposing, however, the pupil answered: "The element of space," meaning that the psychic sense of a stationary (vertical) harmony, or any sequence of harmonies, shifts according to place, as when sounded in a deserted cathedral rather than a crowded chamber.

He would be wrong. For teacher's answer is:

"The element of Time. The question of the time-interval that must elapse between one sound and another if the two sounds are to produce a pleasing consonance or an *interesting* relation, has been avoided."

Pleasing and *interesting* aside, this concept may be less unique than Pound realized, although in 1923 it was stimulating. To his credit he develops (or rather, randomly restates) this notion not with conclusions of eyes, which are only means in music, but always of ears, which are ends. His reactions were dictates of blood circulation, though not the blood of corpses. "Pure theory" (he cites someone named Richter) "can not . . . concern itself with practice." And more deliciously (quoting one Sauzay): *"Il faut se borner à penser que J.-S. Bach écrivait la musique par certains procédés dont la loi générale nous échappe."*

His concern with acoustics was as deeply special as that of, say, Lou Harrison today, yet always (and this is not so frequent as you'd think) as applied to *sound*, the audible glowing of nature as opposed to the "academicism [which] is not excess of knowledge [but] the possession of *idées fixes* as to how one should make use of one's data." Yet in his joy at debunking pedantry he could become pedantic himself ("There is nothing sacred about the duration of the second," etc.), but his ultimate and whimsical wish was to render the physics of sound so complex that composers would grow discouraged, would "give up trying to compose by half-remembered rules, and really listen to sound." How even more welcome today, in the dreary ice of our "serious" musical fray, would be that warm wish come true!

One wonders how the impact of this opening chapter might have resounded were its spontaneous information better coordinated. Then again, coordination might have detracted from the rugged urgency which finally reaches us more as poetry than as knowledge—poetry, as everyone knows, dealing more with word sequence than with idea.

George Antheil. His name to our young is not even a name, and his performances number zero. But yesterday he was not only the self-proclaimed *Bad Boy of Music*—such was titled his autobiography—but the official bad boy (or "leftist," as the avant-garde was then named) of most expatriate twenties intellectuals, the literary ones rather more than the musical. Gertrude Stein received him although she knew nothing of music; Virgil Thomson promoted him both in journalism and in the organization of far-out concerts; James Joyce, a great Purcell fancier, discussed him as the prime mover of the now common machinery-in-art movement, and even considered collaborating with him on an opera; while Hemingway owed to his influential relations the publication of *In Our Time*.

Mr. Pound it was, though, who eventually, for better or worse, immortalized him in the present book. The aging poet's apotheosizing of this very young composer amounts in fact to a conglomeration of bon mots on art, bon mots so occasionally cogent, yet wild, they become impossible to summarize other than by illustration.

Stravinsky is quickly put down in favor of (or, at best, equated to) Antheil:

> Stravinsky arrived as a comfort, but one could not say definitely that his composition was new music; he was a relief from Debussy; but this might have been merely the heritage of Polish folk music manifest in the work of an instinctive genius ... Stravinsky's merit lies very largely in taking hard bits of rhythm, and noting them

with care. Antheil continues this; and these two composers mark a definite break with the "atmospheric"
school; they both write horizontal music. . . .

Why was Stravinsky a comfort? And how—though it
makes little difference—was his composition not "new"?
Certainly he was less a "relief" than (and doubtless he himself would admit it) a *continuation* or outgrowth of Debussy.
It is unclear how Polish music was reflected in this oh-so-
Russian; as for his being horizontal, if one must equate
music to the linear, Stravinsky, at least in the twenties, was
most certainly vertical—that is, harmonic.

Later remarks on Stravinsky provide their own commentary:

> The "Sacre" stands, but its cubes, solid as they are,
> are in proportion to [Antheil's] Ballet Mécanique as
> the proportions of architecture are to those of town
> planning. . . . "Noces" falls to pieces. After the Ballet it
> sounds like a few scraps of Wagner, a Russian chorale
> (quite good), a few scraps of Chopin, a few high notes
> "pianolistic."

Good God! But then Pound is elsewhere correct in main-
taining that the "authentic genius will be as touchy . . .
about the differences between his own particular art and all
others, as, or than, he will about any possible analogies with
the arts."

> Antheil has . . . noted his rhythms with an exactitude,
> which we may as well call genius . . . has purged the
> piano, has made it into a respectable musical instru-

ment. . . . Antheil is probably the first artist to use machines, I mean actual modern machines, without bathos. [There is nowhere mention of Varèse.] I think that music is the art most fit to express the fine quality of machines. Machines are now a part of life. . . . A painting of a machine is like a painting of a painting. The lesson of machines is precision, valuable to the plastic artist, and to the literati. . . .

Then he approvingly quotes Antheil: " 'the failure of Stravinsky [!] . . . In accepting Satie as a master, we see that he [Stravinsky] was nothing but a jolly Rossini.' "

This chapter elsewhere offers such tantalizing propositions as: "Prose is perhaps only half an art . . . you can not get a word back into the non-human." Then it moralizes in a manner so *démodé* that the eyebrows of a Larry Rivers today, or even of a Boulez, would scarcely be raised; while a Frank O'Hara could only agree about longevity as it pertains to artists rather than to their work, artists seldom anymore seeming to care about posterity, or even about the word "art": "The thorough artist is constantly trying to form an ideograph of 'the good' in his art; I mean the ideograph of admirable compound-of-qualities that make any art permanent."

Pound goes on to quote appraisals by Antheil himself, Antheil who notes a "constant tirade against improvisation": "Debussy, soul of ardent virgin, clear and sentimental implanted in great artistic nature." (Ironically, Debussy's own assessment of Grieg, of all people, had not been too unlike this, and—if you will—equally "false": he compared the Norwegian's music to the sounds heard in old folks' homes, to the taste of bonbons stuffed with snow!)

Antheil is finally defined by Pound as "possibly the first

American or American-born musician to be taken seriously
... [who] has made a beginning; that is, in writing music
that couldn't have been written before."

Since any composer worthy of the name, be he "conservative" or "experimental," writes music that, by definition,
couldn't have been written before, Antheil's fellow musicians
of this period were mostly a good deal more resistant to
him than were the authors. He himself, a few years later,
whether by abandon or ousting or nostalgia, quit the French
musical scene for California, where he continued to turn out
vast amounts of not-too-often-played scores (influenced no
less by machines than by Hedy Lamarr, to whom his *Heroes
of Today* is dedicated), and to write journalism on subjects
quite unrelated to his field. In 1959 he died in comparative
obscurity, and to date his music has not been revived by
either Right or Left.

What did Antheil himself think of Pound's overly personal, often disordered and irrelevant, yet sycophantic précis
of his *oeuvre?* In the postwar retrospect of 1945 he tells us.

> It seems terribly unfair of me, at this time, to pro-
> ceed to criticize Ezra Pound, now that the poet has
> fallen into disgrace. But, I emphasize, I would write
> these pages exactly this way if Ezra had become an
> international hero instead. For from the first day I met
> him Ezra was never to have the slightest idea of what I
> was really after in music. I honestly don't think he
> wanted to have. I think he merely wanted to use me
> as a whip with which to lash out at all those who dis-
> agreed with him, particularly Anglo-Saxons; I would be
> all the more effective in this regard because I was an
> "unrecognized American."

And he beautifully adds: "The main clues of a composer's life are in his music; but it is not always so easy to read them."

And how do Antheil's surviving peers esteem him? Well, listen, for instance, to the 1967 assessment by Peter Yates, who, in my opinion, is now America's leading spokesman for twentieth-century music:

> . . . the young American George Antheil [took] what then seemed the obvious course of using noise without exploring it. Antheil's explanations after the event tried to rationalize a successful headline-seeking stunt into a considered esthetic achievement. In fact, it was most successful in its headlines. The sound lacks variety; the typewriters used for instruments do not compete effectively with the several pianos; the pianos are borrowed from Stravinsky's far more successful use of them in *The Wedding*; the airplane propeller is no more than Strauss's wind-machine in *Don Quixote*; and the rattling and banging of the percussive elements do not combine to produce musical substance. Similar faults are evident in much of the noise-music which has been composed since that time. Antheil's superficiality became more evident in later compositions, imitating the surfaces of more competent composers.

Or listen to the Britisher Wilfrid Mellers, who (partly from the objectivity that springs from physical distance, partly from the subjectivity of a truly devoted love for us) in 1965 published *Music in a New Found Land*, the most definitive book to date on American music:

> . . . Antheil claims that [*Ballet mécanique*] is built mathematically on the Time-Space concept, like musi-

cal engineering, or modern architecture in sound. He
admits that Varese preceded him in this concept. In
any case, compared with the works of Stravinsky and
Varèse, *Ballet mécanique* has only historical, not musical interest.... [He] used arithmetical durations of
silence as early as 1924, partly as a result of studying
Oriental music.... [However] the work's motor
rhythms relate it to Western music, and it does not get
far with the space-time concept.

Or to the 1966 avowal of a personal sponsor from their
mutual heyday, Virgil Thomson, who presumably needs no
introduction:

> My estimate (in 1926) of him as "the first composer
> of our generation" might have been justified had it
> not turned out eventually that for all his facility and
> ambition there was in him no power of growth. The
> "bad boy of music" ... merely grew up to be a good
> boy. And the *Ballet mécanique,* written before he
> was twenty-five, remains his most original piece.

Like the pseudonymous Monsieur Croche behind whom
Debussy hid, like Bernard Shaw's Corno di Bassetto, indeed
like many a nineteenth-century critic who, for one or another
reason (usually to protect professional status) adopted a
false cognomen, Ezra Pound from 1917 to 1920 wrote fort-
nightly in the *New Age* under the pen name of William
Atheling. In 1923 these admittedly badly written musical
"shiftings" were submitted to Antheil, who bestrewed them
with marginalia. This conjointed enterprise constitutes the
third, and probably most personal, portion of Pound's
treatise. Most personal—partly because Antheil's italicized
interpolations are fairly incidental agreements and none too

witty (examples: "A bad musician will only admit a name so well-known that there can be no question about it. He is a bad musician because he has no 'guts' anyway"; or, commenting on a remark that the British concert performer is chosen from the exclusively eviscerated strata of the community: "How funny it must be in England"; or: "I bow gracefully"; or simply: "Bravo! !"), and partly because here Pound expounds on what instinctively a great poetical layman can most "know" about: performance (as opposed to composition), and what he terms the "musicking" of verse, namely prosody.

A telling wisdom careens in the wake of platitude: "Hundreds of musical careers have been muddled because performers have not understood how entirely music must lead its own life; must have its own separate existence apart from the audience. . . ." Then: "An era of bad taste probably gathers to itself inferior matter from preceding periods. An indiscriminate rummaging in the past does not help to form a tradition."

Still, when talking of words and music, he deserves quotation in any (but there *aren't* any!—except my own, and I didn't know Pound then) manual on how to make a song:

> There are different techniques in poetry; men write to be read, or spoken, or declaimed, or rhapsodized; and quite differently to be sung. Words written in the first manners are spoiled by added music; it is superfluous; it swells out their unity into confusion. When skilled men write for music then music can both render their movement . . . tone by tone, and quantity by quantity; or the musician may apparently change the word-movement with a change that it were better to call a realization. Music is not speech. Arts attract us because they

are different from reality. Emotions shown in actual speech poured out in emotion will not all go into verse. The printed page does not transmit them, nor will musical notation record them phonographically.

Thematic invention in music has coincided with periods when musicians were intent on poetry, intent on the form and movement of words. Thematic invention is the weakest spot in contemporary music *everywhere*. The rhythms of French are less marked, but only in France do we find a careful study of the verbal qualities. I do not think I have shown any delirious or unbalanced appreciation of the modern French, but among their song-setters are practically the only contemporary song-setters whom one can respect.

The best poets have been nature poets only incidentally. Nature appears here and there in their work, but is not singled out for their subject-matter. Whatever "religion and Christianity" may still mean to the populace and to the modern heath-dweller, religion as exploited by artists of the last century has been mostly exploited as convenient furniture and not from any inner necessity.

One might take exception to other of his songwriting generalities:

The perfect song occurs when the poetic rhythm is in itself interesting, and when the musician augments, illumines it, without breaking away from, or at least without going too far from the dominant cadences and accents of the words; when ligatures illustrate the verbal qualities, and the little descants and prolongations fall in with the main movements of the poem.

Still we will all agree that

> In the finest lyrics the music comes from the words and so enriches, reinforces, illuminates them. We will recapture this art of illuminating only when we have musicians capable of literary discrimination, capable of selecting *cantabile* words, and of feeling the fine shades of their timbre, of their minor hurries and delays.

Other jewels can also be detached from their setting and thrown out loose here:

> Our decadence may be due to the fact that the educated are now too stupid to participate in the arts.
> You cannot compare Music since Beethoven with the early thin music which is like delicate patterns on glass. Since Beethoven people have thought of music as of something with a new bulk and volume.
> One must, perhaps, find one's ideal artists in fragments, never whole and united.
> Tchaikowsky: a certain cheapness is imminent in this composer. He is not cheap all the time, or even, perhaps, most of the time but he keeps one in a state of anxiety.

Occasionally there is a gaffe like "We noticed how *stupid* Liszt was, and how little he knew about chords" (if Liszt didn't know about chords, nobody did), followed by facile banality like "opera is a diffuse form . . . made to cover light after-dinner conversation," followed by pedantic advice like "It is a good thing for singers to get off the beaten track and hunt up music that is lying in desuetude." (Most music lying in desuetude lies there because God—meaning Lack of Talent—willed it so.)

Special divisions in a similarly inconsistent genre are devoted to the piano (called pye-ano), to the fiddle, the lieder school ("which is wrong"), to ballet, to Chopin and Scriabin and Mozart; and deep in the morass shines a gemlike essay on Oriental music as compared to Provençal poetry.

The whole comes off as a succinct cluster of aphoristic Gallic *pensées* translated into the grouchiest Americanese.

"Varia" gives us more of the same, though it is chiefly directed toward composers. The bulk originally appeared in the *New Masses* and in the *New Criterion*.

Composers are all too aware of being at "the mercy of the executant, and the executant is at the mercy of his endocrines," but they may be amused to see their craft reduced to "knowing what note you want; how long you want it held; and how long one is to wait for the next note, and in making the correct signs for these durations." Pound smartly adds that "it is for lack of just such simple statements . . . that the misunderstandings arise between the musician and the well wisher"; then, for the first time in the whole book, qualifies his authority: ". . . apart from accommodating notes to words, I am an incompetent amateur."

This very amateurism led this very professional Idaho poet, while he was overwhelming world scholarship, to wish to do as much for musical art. That wish was therefore to prove that George Antheil had taken, "or at any rate [had] found a means that can take, music out of the concert hall." This removal presumably would disseminate formal sound throughout an even vaster world than his own literary one and bestow it upon the people as tribal ceremonies had been bestowed in the past, or sea chanties or labor songs. Such has ultimately occurred, moreover, for better or worse, through our John Cage, who would be pleased to read that the "aesthete goes to a factory ... and hears *noise,* and goes away horrified; ... the composer hears noise, but he tries to (?) 'see' (no, no), he tries to *hear* what kind of noise it is." Indeed, Antheil *had* talked vaguely of "tuning up" whole cities, of "silences twenty minutes long *in the form,*" etc., though never put these functions to the test.

Antheil, by our witness today and by his admission yesterday, served as sacrificial goat for a genius whose *gauche prévoyance* had, in itself, little influence, but was in fact an image of what, distortedly, would come to pass. If for no other reason then, Pound's treatise is worth a re-perusal in the sixties. For strange as it may seem, few scholars know of this book though they've hazily heard of Pound's opera, while few musicians know of the opera though they've hazily heard of this book.

Any jottings of the Great (Pound was and is great)—even a *billet-doux* or laundry list (and this volume is much more than that)—become, by definition, important, deserving the concentration of cultured laymen and all other fellow artists.

13 · Ravel

Of those composers I most love, Ravel is the single one through whose sound I feel the man himself. The feeling can rise straight from a harmony hit in passing, evoking within a split second the vastly nonabstract realm of Paris before I was born: my heart beats in a *salon faubourien* during conversation with an artist I never met in a time that is not, and real tears well up for the unknown which is hyper-familiar. Time and again this happens as I'm seated at the piano playing Ravel, or hearing him in a concert hall. No other composer pulls quite the same trick.

A century ago (on the hundredth anniversary of Jane Austen's birth) Ravel was born of solvent and understanding parents in the village of Ciboure near the Spanish frontier. These few facts color all that he became. His art straddled the border as it straddled centuries, being in texture as opulent as a tourist's notion of Iberia, in shape as pristine as Rameau, in intent no less modern than ragas or group therapy, and in subject matter mostly antiromantic. Listen again to *Bolero*. ("It's my masterpiece," said the composer. "Unfortunately it contains no music.") French logic drenched in Basque mystery.

Mysterious for its lack of mystery was his worldly life: he didn't read much, didn't carouse, had avuncular crushes and a juvenile taste for enamel toys, heavy spices, mother figures, Siamese cats. Beneath garish shirts lay bland discretion.

But the unknown is good press. (Which is why a Maurice Sachs, dilettantish and mediocre, still holds the boards in France: his death was a publicized enigma, like Poe's, Lorca's, Desnos'.) The two most frequent questions on Ravel: Was he Jewish? Was he homosexual? (One assumes he couldn't be both.) Nobody knows so everyone cares. Beyond this—and beyond the details of his long, sad agony —the man was less absorbing than the artist. But the artist's method has been finely documented. What to add? This musician, who over the years brought me more than any other, now leaves me at a loss. What we love we long to share but need to hoard.

What we learn as children we question without question. That Ravel's music was standoffish, elegant, well made and casual I took as fact like the Oedipus complex or Eliot's genius, wondering uneasily why that special sound entered me like a heady draft of carnality throttling my Quaker frame to dwell on love and the pursuit of happiness.

It was the summer of 1936 that I first heard him, on the antimacassared upright in Oberlin. While kohlrabi fumes floated from the pantry, my cousin Kathleen performed the *Sonatine*, which awakened me forever. Thinking the composer's name was Reville, I could locate no more of his music.

By 1937 I knew the spelling plus every work on record. I'd even begun composing a bit of Ravel myself.

On December 28, a Tuesday brimming with sunshine, Father (I still picture him there on the sofa) read aloud from the Chicago *Tribune:* "French Composer Dies." (His name didn't yet merit a headline.) Gershwin had gone that summer. Now this. Moved, I sat down and played the *Pavane*. "How obvious," snorted a fourteen-year-old pal when I told him later.

Like Minerva he emerged full-blown. Like Chopin he did not "advance," have periods, grow more complex. He entered the world with the true artist's faculty for self-appraisal, and all his life wrote the same kind of music, consistently good. Goodness accounts, as with Chopin, for a proportionately short catalogue. Virginity accounts, as with Minerva, for concern about fertility through craft.

Unlike Chopin he was no contrapuntalist. His canonic forays are abortive: those thousand examples of balanced clean lines are not counterpoints but harmonic shorthand. That fugue in *Le Tombeau de Couperin* is idiosyncratic.

A nation's music resembles its language in all respects, and since French is the only European tongue with no rhythm (no tonic accent), any metricalization of a French phrase in music can be construed as correct. Lacking natural pulse, all French music becomes impressionist. French composers when they opt for rhythm exploit it squarely, like children. The spell of *Bolero* resides in its nonvariety, its contrast to Gallic speech which inherently rejects hypnosis, as opposed to American speech which like jazz is pure monotony. (Not for nothing was hypnosis first documented by a Frenchman, Charcot. Where rhythm is a stranger, rhythm is a prophet.)

Bolero has nothing to do with French music, yet only a Frenchman could have composed it.

Ravel's signatures are harmony and tune. His melodies are based on, and emerge from, chords. His identity (like Puccini's) lies in long line.

Melody is horizontal. No matter how brief or fragmental, melody necessarily unfolds, and so is experienced in time. Like sex and food, melody can be enjoyed in the Now. We react to a tune as it happens, although (unlike sex and food) we cannot judge the tune until it is over, whether the tune is three notes of Webern or three pages of liturgical chant.

Harmony is vertical. Harmony too may exist in time (a single chord may be indefinitely sustained), although that is not its defining signal. (A shifting series or progression of chords is just that: chords, not *chord*—harmonies, not harmony.) Of course, a progression of simultaneous tunes—counterpoint, as it's named—produces at all moments harmony, that is, vertical noises that result from (but aren't specifically the purpose of) the juxtaposition of moving lines; but these moments are actually points in space rather than in time: no sooner sounded than they perish, or are retained like antimatter only in memory, in the past, while melody is experienced solely in the present, like a movie.

Debussy never, not once, even for violins, composed extended melody. His vocal writing, though tuneful, is glorified recitative, while the occasional *grande ligne* hints in his orchestral work are either cut short in mid-orgasm or exhaust themselves too soon for logic. (That brief outburst in *Iberia*'s middle movement brings no "expected" relief, merely dribbles off.) Such Debussyan tunes as are lengthy, like the vast ending of *La Mer* or in the soaring *Etudes*, are additive: literal repetitions piled up like pancakes.

Not that he couldn't melodize, but he had other fish to fry. The music of Debussy, that famed roué, leads somewhere, but not to sex. The music of Ravel, that presumed abstainer, usually emulates bodily fulfillment.

We know of Debussy's love-hate of Wagner. But how did a nonlinear type like him react to such limitless ropes of silk as Ravel wove for his dragonfly fiddles in *L'Enfant et les sortilèges*, or to the endless opening theme of *Daphnis et Chloé*, or to that unbroken languor of the solo flute? Do we admire in others what we too can do, or what we cannot?

Ravel and Debussy each had a strong personality and so were inimitable; but they were contemporaries, after all, bearing the same age relationship as Liszt to Franck, or as Copland to Barber. (Satie, whom we think of as Papa, actually lay between them like Lucky Pierre.) Once we agree it's unfair to compare them, it's fun to compare them.

Their color is abundant and varied, but always pure. The difference between French and German orchestration is that the former uses no doubling. Reinforcement, yes; but where in Strauss a string tune is thickened with winds or brass, in Ravel the fat is skimmed off and held in abeyance. This makes for what is known as *transparent* instrumentation—a sound paradoxically opulent and lean. By extension the sound applies to his piano solo and vocal works. Sumptuous bones.

Another unchallenged *donnée*: Ravel's taste, the good

taste—*son goût exquis*—which we accept at face value along with his "sophisticated" wit.

What *is* taste (or wit, for that matter) in music? For programmatic pieces it can be defined, but can the definition be extended (like the orchestral transparency of his piano works) to abstract pieces?

If taste means decorum, boundary, *mesure*, then Ravel's jeweled box holds jewels, Debussy's jeweled box holds a heart. But to a Mahler that heart is candy, to a Puccini it's gall.

Yes, he had taste. Like all Frenchmen Ravel was blinded by Poe, whose essay *The Philosophy of Composition* influenced him (he claimed) more than any music; yet he never actually envisaged setting Poe's fiction, as Debussy had planned with the "Fall of the House of Usher." Like all Frenchmen Ravel was approached by the gaudy Ida Rubinstein, whose spoken voice (that least musical of instruments, in contrast to the singing voice) was the requisite solo for the works she commissioned; yet he never succumbed to using that voice, as Debussy did in his *Martyre*.

Alone, subject matter determines taste in music. (Music without subject matter cannot be argued as tasteful or tasteless, there are no criteria.) Murder, war, and amorous passion being the texts for nine-tenths of lyric theater, and such texts being beyond taste, most opera is tasteless. Again, Ravel was tasteful there: his sonorous stories never grazed grown-up matters except in parody (licentious doings in *L'Heure espagnole*) or from a safe distance (slave revolt in *Chansons madécasses*). Otherwise he stayed close to home, which is to say close to the nonsexual side of Colette. Nor did he ever, save for a brief minute in the early song *Sainte* on a poem of Mallarmé, musicalize even a quasi-religious verse: the gods forbid such breech of taste.

Yet who does not forget himself at *L'Enfant et les sortilèges?* Colette's very stage directions are high poetry, and contribute to making this my single most preferred work of the century. Why? Because despite its length the quality of inspiration remains appropriately fevered while exploiting (no less adroitly than Bach's passions and Wagner's dramas do) each aspect of sonorous speech: instrumental opulence, both solo and orchestral, and vocal expertise, both solo and choral.

(Ravel and Colette, as inevitable a pair as Gilbert and Sullivan, scarcely knew each other.)

How unfair to accuse him of taste! To hear *Daphnis et Chloé* is to hear great art (despite the hideous heavenly choirs, so copied by sound tracks that we hear the original now as a copy), but to see the score is to blush. Each "telling" tune illustrates a mawkish stage direction: the violas pose a question to which the shepherd opens his arms, the harp sweeps upward as the lovers reunite, etc.—what we call Mickeymousing.

Apropos, after Ravel's death his brother, witnessing his first animated cartoon, declared, "That's how *L'Enfant et les sortilèges* should be mounted," a declaration echoed by many another tasteful Frenchman. (Disney is second to Poe on France's short list of esteemed Americans.) *L'Enfant* should never be mounted in any form; like *Saint Matthew Passion* the work's tightness is too elaborately delicate to support visuals.

(As for wit, who can define wit either, as it relates to non-vocal music?)

Influences we avow are, of course, the conscious ones— those we're sure don't show. Once assimilated, the property becomes ours. Magnanimously we admit the theft, safely knowing that no one detects the original beneath our paint.

(Unconscious influence alone is damning.) Thus Ravel announces Saint-Saëns, Schubert, Mozart as his progenitors. Who would guess it?

His influence on others? On Poulenc it is obvious, though no one ever points out the harmonic progression of three chords in Ravel's L'Indifférent (1905) pilfered intact fifty years later to form the motto of Poulenc's Carmélite opera. More interestingly, no one ever points out the cadenza for two clarinets in Ravel's Rapsodie espagnole (1908) pilfered intact three years later to form the motto for Stravinsky's Petrouchka ballet. That bitonal Petrouchka sound outlined Stravinsky's harmony for the next decade, and by extension most Western music for the next half-century, yet the sound demonstrably stems from a few casual bars in the French musician's pseudo-Spanish idiom.

He evolutionized keyboard virtuosity more than anyone since Liszt, yet his complete solo piano works fit comfortably into one evening's program.

In his sixty-two years, Ravel, who worked constantly, didn't turn out more than eight hours' worth of music, as contrasted to Debussy's sixteen, Beethoven's thirty, Wagner's fifty, Bach's seventy, Ives's two thousand or Webern's two. Of those eight hours none is slipshod or routine. Not that he was a miniaturist; he was a perfectionist. So was Bach a perfectionist—different times, different mores—but a page of Ravel orchestration is twenty times busier than a page of Bach's. (Still, since Stravinsky was twice as busy as Ravel, yet twice as prolific, we draw no conclusions.)

He was a classicist, yes, sometimes, in those square-structured suites, concertos and pastiches with their recapitulations and so-called symmetrical melodies. (Symmetrical is a poor word, since time cannot have symmetry.) But so many other pieces are truly impressionist—all of Gaspard *de la nuit*, most of *Miroirs*, many of the straight orchestra numbers (though none of the thirty-three songs, curiously, since songs, being based on words, are by definition musically free). Such pieces are not so much heard as overheard, come upon, already transpiring before they start, evanescent. Made solely of middles, without beginnings or ends, they emerge from nowhere, from a mist, trouble us for a dazzling while, then without notice vanish like Scarbo, fade like Ondine. Any of these sparklers could be convincing shorter or convincing longer for they have been spinning always, and will always continue, though within human earshot only for those fugitive minutes.

How to perform such pieces! Not, certainly, like the composer himself, with nineteenth-century mushiness, sabotaging the perfect interplay of his puzzles. Vague sounds, to make their point, need precise rendition, just as white on a canvas needs additional pigments to have meaning as white. Play what you see, the notes will take care of themselves. Add no nuances, they are imbedded in the score—not, to be sure, as verbal indications but as notated musical calculations. (Yet my heart sinks regularly when baritones, reaching the closing bars of the air to Dulcinée, slow down the meter along with the rhythm: Ravel scored a ritard by elongating note values, not by writing the word "ritard.")

He needs no interpretation; he should be played like Bach, the way Gieseking played him. (Bach takes interpretation; he should be played like Ravel, the way Landowska played him.)

I have wanted to disqualify what is often claimed and to add what is seldom said. So I have not bothered to mention that Ravel was five feet tall or that he never married. I used to know people whom Ravel knew well (soprano Madeleine

Grey, violinist Hélène Jourdan-Morhange, composer Roland-Manuel), but none ever revealed much about the man or about his musical attitudes. Today they are dead, Ravel is a hundred, and facts about him grow as unreachable as facts about Shakespeare.

Having touched on all variables of music as they pertained to Ravel, let me recall them quickly:

His rhythmic sense, characteristically French, is vague, except where consciously italicized.

He made no pretense at being a contrapuntalist, and his few stabs at canon (with the exception of the ecstatic false fugue at the close of *L'Enfant*) are banal.

He was a harmonist born. His harmonies, both in their vertical selves and in sequence, contain the inevitability of greatness, are almost embarrassingly tactile, and are always recognizable as his despite their providing the unique base for all chordal progressions in pop music internationally for fifty years.

His tunes, spun out for mile upon silver mile, locate him in a camp far from Beethoven or even Debussy, both of whom glued together (always ingeniously) their truncated fragments.

His instrumental hues (again characteristically French) are unadulterated. But if the French have always been noted for economical means, which in turn are the roots of taste, no one has ever focused on taste in, say, Franck or Fauré.

What is called Ravel's wit is his removal, when choosing texts to set, from sober adult romance. (But is the anguished *Trio* witty? And who finally dares call it or any music anguished?)

The effects of his music, assumed to be restrained and upper-class (so as to distinguish them easily from Debussy's), are really nonintellectual and replete with voluptuous yearn-ing. These effects were as fully realized in his earliest works as in his last, in his impressionist pieces as in his formal ones —the latter being, ironically, more "physical" than the former if only because (unlike Debussy) they relied on sonata form, which is the standard musical emulation of sexual intercourse.

The more we know someone's music the more we know how it should *not* go. Distance is not imitated by softness. If, for example, the more impressionistic of Ravel's piano pieces sound as though they were being eavesdropped upon —like something we become aware of as being whispered downstairs—then they must project. Projection comes through precision, the articulation of musical syntax, which is always crystal clear on Ravel's printed page.

Even without his music the thought of him makes me feel good.

Nobody dislikes Ravel, and nobody disapproves. Can that be said of any other musician?

14 · Poulenc

He is among the magic few. Without his art my world would weigh less. Any severities which now follow are the critiques of love.

If musical greatness, as Rimbaud claimed, is exclusive of innovation, then Francis Poulenc was a genius. If real artists, as Radiguet claimed, have their own voice and so need only to copy to prove their individuality, then Poulenc dignified the crime of plagiarism. And no composer of the past century, the only century in which originality was ever equated —by peasant and poet alike—with quality, was less concerned than Poulenc with originality.

Originality is a hollow virtue; everything's new under the sun. If to be novel were to be fresh and inventive and dramatic, Spohr would grab prizes from Wagner, Rebikov would drown Debussy in ninths, Schoenberg would expose Berg as an amateur theatricalist.

Poulenc was more than merely influenced: he rifled intact the treasure of others. This was once common practice (Bach-Vivaldi), and Poulenc revived the practice, a risky one for those few minor musicians who used him as model only to discover he was no model at all. For his practice was an end, not a beginning; like all strong artists he did not open doors but closed them.

He was a converse dybbuk. Using no mask, he sang through his own lips with other men's voices. His very lack of originality became the unabashed signature of unique glories.

The premise of unoriginality, it seems to me, must smooth the ground for any "original" assessment of Poulenc's current value. That ground, fertilized by music's five variables— melody, harmony, counterpoint, rhythm (the only component to exist by itself), and instrumentation—was plowed by the composer in his way—the way of pastiche which bloomed into personality.

Melody. Does that word recall him? In the purely Puccinian sense of soaring sweep, Poulenc was no melodist at all. Though his fame was largely vocal, and vocal supposedly means tuneful, offhand his only sweep that comes to mind is orchestral: the *2-Piano Concerto*'s second theme, the one that sounds like "Jeepers Creepers." And even those nine swooning notes, like Debussy's *fausses grandes lignes* (in contrast to the true long lines of, say, Ravel's *Daphnis*), dissolve before they evolve.

Singers never say "my voice," they say "the voice," as though that voice led its own life, which in a way it does. A voice's beauty, even its intelligence, are not entirely related to the intelligence and beauty of the singer. When singers refer to "gracious writing for the voice" they don't always imply ecstatic Gregorian (Puccinian) flow, and this is something Poulenc realized more than any other voice writer. His prosody—in song, in chorus, in opera—is declamatory, one note to a syllable. Such little melisma as exists specifically within *Dialogues des Carmélites* is not in the French but in the Latin tongue, as at the start of the *Ave Maria*. (In 1963 when Frank O'Hara and I collaborated on a song for the Poulenc Memorial, my accompaniment was a literal quote from that *Ave Maria*. Don't tell anyone.) If melodic meant poetic license—the stretching of a word beyond normal spoken length, and thus beyond comprehension—then a Boulez would be more melodic than Poulenc. The latter may well be the most sung French composer of the past fifty years, but (or rather, because) his word settings are more verbal than vocal.

His tunes—usually they are true tunes, not recitations—stem from speech; he never squeezed verse into prewritten musical phrases. His concern for correct stress made even his lushest songs talky. Since most of those songs are composed on strict rhymed meter, and since the composer's instinctive language is diatonic, a formal squareness results which extends even to his opera recitatives on free prose. By further extension his instrumental pieces become, at heart, word settings from which the words are removed.

He liked to think of his prosodic excesses as perverse, though in fact they are superdescriptive. How wickedly pleased he felt, after hours of struggle, about a decision to distort and thereby to heighten the word *agonie* by agogically hitting the central syllable (although the French language, having no inherent tonic accent, would not call for such a stress) when Blanche, near the end of the second tableau, declares that were she to become a nun she would like to be named ". . . *soeur Blanche de l'Agonie du Christ!*" This is the kind of detail which Francis Poulenc, the social man, with the catholicity of selection that total self-involvement seems to allow, used to recount not only to musical peers, but to a countess or a concierge. And the countess and the concierge listened.

Take Chopin's dominant sevenths, Ravel's major sevenths, Fauré's straight triads, Debussy's minor ninths, Mussorgsky's augmented fourths. Filter them, as Satie did, through the added sixth chords of vaudeville (which the French called Le Music Hall), blend in a pint of Couperin to a quart Stravinsky, and you get the harmony of Poulenc.

He laid eggs like a cuckoo in all nests but his own, yet every nestling warbled pure Francis.

Ravel's *Une barque sur l'océan* is a lesser work by a major composer. Poulenc's *Figure humaine* is a major work by a lesser composer—or one who used to be termed lesser. One section from the major work, named *Toi ma patiente*, is a note-for-note steal from *Une barque*: tune, key, rhythm, chords, all. And yet Poulenc's choral working-out is superior to Ravel's piano piece precisely because it *is* a working-out.

Dialogues starts right out with what may be labeled "Blanche's theme," borrowed from Poulenc's own *Messe*, a work pure as holy water. With each reference to Blanche's father, whom she loves irreproachably, or when the father himself reflects upon his dutiful past, the theme flows through a chord sequence borrowed from Ravel's *L'Indifférent*, a work carnal as sweat.

Poulenc's dedication of *Dialogues* to Claude Debussy "who gave me the taste for writing music" may be precautionary. The Mother Superior's long allusion in prison to Christ in the Olive Grove is pitched over a chord sequence invented by Debussy for Saint Sebastian's long allusion to the Wounded Laurel.

Play the last twenty-nine bars of Act I, and ask someone to guess what Puccini opera they're from.

Counterpoint is no more an ingredient of Poulenc than of any French composer between 1900 and 1945. Only when compelled, as in unaccompanied choral works, does he concoct minor elaborations in the fifth species. But never even an abortive canon, much less a fugue. Exquisite and satisfying though his polyphony be, it always serves the means to a harmonic end.

Few of his time signatures denote other than a simple three or a simple four, and their metrical subdivisions contain no eccentricity. Yet he cannily bent those straight angles —circling the square, so to speak—through pulse.

Some French composers, for instance Duparc, write only what's inherently slow: their fast music is really slow music played fast. Others, for instance Honegger, write only what's inherently fast: their slow music is really fast music played slow. Still others, like Franck, write always moderato. Now, Poulenc's music at all speeds seems born to its velocity, as though his very heartbeat, like a metronome, could readjust to several basic outlooks.

He enriched that plainest of all rhythmic devices, the ostinato. Observe *La Carpe*, the last little song in the nineteen-year-old's first cycle, *Le Bestiaire*, based on quatrains of Apollinaire. *La Carpe*'s ten limpid measures are as much a master's-piccc (if not a chef d'oeuvre) as the whole of *Fidelio*, since both are at once self-contained and infinite—they could go on forever. Two, and only two, chords, always displacing each other, are nonetheless welded by the once-stated melody in the voice, and their implicit monotony is made interesting by that slow-flipping tail in the left hand. Indeed, the accompaniment is not an accompaniment but a piano solo with a vocal obbligato, endlessly repeated, a solo leading nowhere like those centenarian carp themselves, jewels with a single perfect facet, spawned under Louis Quatorze and still swimming at Versailles.

(As one idly ponders the vast lost branches from Djuna's *Nightwood* excised and discarded by T. S. Eliot, so one dreams of the castaway songs from the *Bestiaire*. Once there were twelve. At the suggestion of Georges Auric, whose advice Poulenc sought regarding his every piece during forty years, six were scrapped. In 1955 for Marya Freud's birthday Poulenc did come up with another animal poem, *La Souris*, from the Apollinaire collection. Was it new or a rewrite? Auric meanwhile had a more cultured but less adventuresome eye than his friend. The same eye he turned on Poulenc's music after the fact was turned on his own before the fact; intellect inhibited creativity. If Poulenc sometimes regretted giving forth, Auric regretted holding back.)

Ostinato was the one method, more than any other, which Poulenc used in order to make a piece go. It could be argued that he "thought ostinato" even when not actually employing it, which accounts for the unchromatic sameness of much of his work in all tempos. Ostinato colored his whole life, since, like Ravel or Matisse, though unlike Debussy or Picasso, he was born mature, never progressed or had "periods," but spoke always the same musical language, in both big and short forms. (His know-how predated his technique. The manuscript of the *Bestiaire*, of all cycles the most sophisticated, was so naively notated—with triple flats and such—that the proofs had to be reengraved.)

His career ever more openly declared its derivations. One cannot quite put a finger on the source of *La Carpe*, but the source of Poulenc's last great ostinato is thrillingly (I almost wrote disastrously) transparent. If the *Salve Regina* which frames the whole last scene of *Dialogues* did not exist Stravinsky would have had to invent it—and did, thirty years earlier, for *Oedipus Rex*. Stravinsky's iterated triplet—three repeated notes which then rise a minor third to three repeated notes which then fall back a minor third, which then rise again, then fall back, then rise, then fall, eternal, hypnotic—become, *chez* Poulenc, duplets performing the same function, that of tensing a loose vocal line chanted by doomed comrades. Stravinsky's rhythmic *trouvaille* in its maddening simplicity is dangerously famous. But what exonerates his imitator from the charge of mere mimicry is this: whereas Stravinsky keeps his ground bass unmodulating and never doubles the "accompanying" tune, Poulenc slowly hauls the tonal center upward and adorns his melody with strings. *Salve Regina* becomes a French scaffold built from Russian wood, and the most affecting decor in all opera. Fifteen women move single file toward their death. With each horrendous crunch of the blade one voice drops out and the music changes key, until finally Constance intones the theme alone, perceives Blanche making her way through the crowd, smiles with faith, dies. Blanche herself then mounts the stairs and the opera ends.

So intense is the last moment that we ignore a plot defect: Blanche's name is not on the headsman's list. It is unlikely that a woman who elbows her way haphazardly to the block will get her head chopped off—and without missing a beat—just because she wants it that way. *N'est pas martyre qui veut*.

Some contend (the late Peter Yates among them) that the offstage guillotine distracts from the music, when precisely the guillotine *is* the music, and far more integral than, say, the noise of Satie's typewriters in *Parade*.

In the game of pigeonholing composers by timbre—where Chopin is identified as a piano, Bach a violin, Beethoven a string quartet, Debussy an orchestra with nothing doubled, Strauss an orchestra with everything doubled, Palestrina a choir, Hindemith a brass band, Stravinsky a drum with viola, Puccini a soprano with cello, Weber a white clarinet, Delius an amber bassoon, and Martinu (as Clurman once described him) a Chinese nightclub under water—Poulenc turns into an oboe (although he looked like a trumpet). Why not a human voice? Because his nature is the oboe, a nature transferred to other mediums. Why not a piano? Because he composed so graciously for keyboard the composition was weak, like much of Rachmaninoff's which sounds less composed than improvised, and improvisation is a one-shot deal so far as lasting effect is concerned. It's only a game.

Yet demonstrably Poulenc was more at home with woodwinds than with brass or strings or percussion. He contributed nothing to the straight symphonic repertory. His ballets and concertos (except the one for organ) are seldom played. His orchestration, such as we hear it through the operas and the three chorus-and-orchestra pieces, is skillful and clean, always "sounds," always reinforces, but has no profile, runs no risks, never interferes. Like the pre-Romantics, his strings are mostly fill-in, his brass mostly fanfare, his battery all backup with no independence. Only his winds, which he treats (as Britten sometimes does) in the cantabile style that most composers reserve for bowed instruments, take on life of their own. But, among his chamber works, the sonatas for solo strings are hopelessly trite because he lives too close for comfort to the corn inherent in all strings. When he feeds this corn, at one remove, to winds, he finds his true milieu. Were you to object that his milieu is the human voice, I would agree, for he treats voices like woodwinds and woodwinds like voices. Were I a teacher I'd ask my Poulenc-singing pupils to emulate an oboe. Every song he ever wrote, with slight nudging here and there, "tells" on the instrument.

Neither of Poulenc's two most convincing vocal interpreters has a "real" voice of the kind that transports opera buffs. Yet Denise Duval was (except for Callas) the world's best postwar singing actress. Her greatness, like Pierre Bernac's, lay in intelligence. She contained the contagious vulnerability of all memorable performers; it wasn't the sound of her curving tunes but her *way* with curving tunes, her comprehension of words, her knowledge of her native language (the only one she ever sang in), and her eyes the size of Garbo's which could depict total innocence or total guilt. As for Bernac, his unlush voice can still sing rings around more lustrous stars. If you don't believe it, compare his homegrown version of *C* or *Hotel* with the touristy renditions by Farrell, Tourel, Kruysen and even Souzay, to see how he crawls inside the notes and inhabits the song.

Poulenc composed three operas. None were collaborations, their librettos being prewritten plays by French authors who were more or less his contemporaries.

The first, *Les Mamelles de Tirésias* (1944), was based on the two-act dadaist farce of Guillaume Apollinaire (1888–1918), whom Poulenc never met, but who was the poet for his earliest songs, *Le Bestiaire* (1918). Concerning women's suffrage and featuring the incomparable Duval, it succeeded where many operas stumble—at filling the audience with true hilarity without compromising the music. Like French operetta of the nineteenth century it was built of set numbers.

The third, *La Voix humaine* (1960), was based on the one-act realist monologue by Jean Cocteau (1889–1963) who was Poulenc's dear friend, and the poet for the composer's second-earliest songs, *Cocardes* (1918). Concerning a woman's suffering and again featuring the divine Duval, it worked where other operas collapse—at keeping recitative from flagging for forty-five minutes. Like no French lyric drama since *Pelléas* it was built solely on speech patterns without set numbers.

Poulenc was faithful to his authors. He musicalized the words of Cocteau (like those of Eluard and Apollinaire) throughout his life, and the two artists died within months of each other.

Whether he ever knew Georges Bernanos I do not know. But between *Mamelles* and *La Voix humaine*, both very profane, brief, and up-to-date, Poulenc commenced, in 1953, composition on that writer's very sacred, lengthy discourse about a tragedy of two centuries ago.

I never read *Last on the Scaffold* by Gertrud von le Fort. I did read and twice saw as a play *Dialogues des Carmélites* which the very Catholic monarchist Bernanos concocted as a movie scenario from the German novel one year before his death in 1948. Bernanos himself did not see his work dramatized, for the movie was never made. But when *Dialogues* was transferred intact to the Paris stage in 1952, the author, who was hitherto known in France as in America mainly through the film of his *Diary of a Country Priest*, became a posthumous celebrity.

To me the play emitted a kind of antiseptic fervor. Protestant, I was both moved by and removed from the nonsexual concerns of the leading character. Blanche de la Force was a fictional aristocrat who, through morose and partly imaginary terror at life's ugliness, entered the convent of Compiègne, only to die an uglier death along with her sisters (actual historical characters) during the early months of the French

Revolution. The drama is less about the revolt than about fear, fear in the absolute: Blanche's introverted hysteria is endemic to all time and place, and, except for the melodramatic finish, it runs a motionless course. Her conversations and those of her mothers and sisters are largely abstract, a bit pietistic, hardly touching on love (except for Christ), much less on the amorousness which ignites nearly every workable opera in history including *Parsifal* and *Suor Angelica*. Not, one might suppose, a text for the *bon vivant* Poulenc. Nor was it his idea.

But when Hervé Dugardin, on behalf of the Milanese house of Ricordi, approached the musician with the project of setting that particular drama to music to be optioned for a premiere at La Scala, Poulenc believed the commission to have been plotted in heaven. If his musical language (as pointed out) never changed syntax over a whole career, his format broadened increasingly. And if his choice of subject matter and medium alternated consciously between profane and sacred, instrumental and vocal, not since 1950 with *Stabat Mater* had he composed a religious work for voices. The time was ripe for what he felt would be his tragic masterpiece.

During those years of the early 1950s I intermittently visited his orange plush apartment, 5 rue de Médicis, overlooking the Luxembourg gardens. After an ample slice of hot homemade mirabelle tart and a cup of camomile garnished with gossip of high carnal vintage, Poulenc would seat himself at the blond-wood piano and bleat the most recent scenes from his work in progress. He sang, like all composers, abominably with zeal, and sounded as he looked: like a maimed cornet, a nasal ferret. But he was the best ensemble pianist I ever heard, his accompaniments for himself, as for others, being a rich exchange of equal rights. (His technique came from one master, Ricardo Viñes, who stressed the paradoxical, and very un-American, procedure of playing cleanly in a flood of pedal—*Le jeu de pédales, ce facteur essentiel de la musique moderne.*)

His interest in me was my interest in him, and I never let him down. Yet I would come away from these meetings with the kind of disappointment which I now recognize as that of the hero-worshiper who makes rules for his hero before the fact. Because Poulenc's most seductive traits had hitherto been those of harmonic opulence and ardent tune, traits utilized even in the pristine *Stabat*, I was bemused, resentful, that he should now forsake them for the new opera's spare, scrubbed texture. *Dialogues des Carmélites* is one of the very rare contemporary masterpieces—Britten's *Death in Venice* is another—whose value and viewpoint were not quickly apparent to me. Is that because I knew them first in a raw state?

The Paris premiere took place on June 21, 1957. The party afterward was at the Dugardins' comfortable mansion, rue de l'Université. There was a buffet for a hundred, though I recall only twenty or so heads—none of the cast—and a mood of cool civility. That was, incidentally, the last time I ever saw Cocteau, who stood aside with Dermit, singularly quiet. He asked me about my *Poet's Requiem* (a choral piece, using a text of his, which Margaret Hillis had conducted in New York the previous February), and I asked him about *Le Testament d'Orphée*, which he was preparing to film. But we did not speak of the opera we had just witnessed (nor, of course, of the fact that he would supply the book for Poulenc's next and final opera, *La Voix humaine*—unless you wish to call *La Dame de Monte Carlo*, a seven-minute monologue on still another playlet of Cocteau's, his final opera). Indeed, no one spoke much of it, despite Poulenc's jocularity. Maybe the reason lay in the production, spartan and understated, in willful contrast to the overblown premiere, in Italian, four months earlier at La Scala. In any case there was no feeling that history had just been made. Yet a month later *Dialogues* was mounted in German in Cologne, in English in San Francisco, and soon after in Rome, Lisbon, Vienna, and on New York television. During no season since then has it remained unperformed somewhere in the world. It is a fact of musical life.

He has been dead fourteen years. Certain composers, when they die, like Hindemith, are placed in cold storage for a generation, sometimes forever. A far smaller group—Bartók, for instance—are no sooner cold than they suffer a resurgence. What Parisian in 1950 would have dreamed that Poulenc, and not Milhaud or Honegger, would eventually be *the* composer to represent his generation? Nor in America was it until after his death that such critics-come-lately as Harold Schonberg, whose business it should be to have known long before, allowed as to how the music wasn't all just perfume and cream. (Though what's wrong with perfume and cream?) But Schonberg is of course wrong to identify Poulenc as nineteenth-century when in fact he's mostly Ravel-Stravinsky.

Twenty years have passed since the Paris premiere and still I'm not sure what to make of *Dialogues*. I never hear it without crying, yet it bores me, which *Pelléas* does not. Flawed it surely is, as all beauty must be. Thus only the lesser, not the leading, characters state the salient points. (Mother Superior: "What God wishes to test is not your strength but your weakness . . ."—a reversible truism. Sister Constance: "We never die for ourselves but for each other, and sometimes in place of each other.") Thus Blanche, as stated earlier, is decapitated without a by-your-leave, while the fate of Mother Marie—she who coerced the nuns to take the martyr's vow—is not pursued. Thus, and especially, although Bernanos' text remains intact, it is in the three inserted Latin liturgies that the composer's muse soars to enter and break the listener's heart. The *Ave Maria*, the *Ave Verum*, and the *Salve Regina*, extraneous to the play, are not only the summits of Poulenc's opera but of French choral music today. Beyond these set numbers there are no ensembles, no duos or trios, certainly no arias, not even for Blanche, although a couple of solos for the Second Mother Superior might be extracted and sung alone one day.

With all the recitative (and he will use still more of it in *La Voix humaine*) one longs for—and suspects that Poulenc may have longed for—a bit more schmaltz and a lot more wit. The play, though touching and even grand, is smug. Poulenc's innate style—that creamy-pop aristocratic style—does not run counter to the "fearsome" plot, and at one brief mention of Paris, when sub rosa he quotes his own so-sly *Mamelles* about that city, we swoon. Poulenc is a tragic humorist, and that isn't always clear here. The Latin sections of *Dialogues* are musically more French than the French sections. The score, after all, is modern, and the text is modern too, even though about the past. But the overall tone is, if not exactly dated, really quite old-fashioned, and so would seem to require more old-fashioned tricks of the opera trade.

In a sense, Poulenc was too honest. The piece is filled with stuffing, albeit lean stuffing, which may be inspired, and perhaps even truly religious. But one waits and waits for it to pass so as to reach those lewd lush tiny tuneful seconds when he lets himself go.

These paragraphs, in a condensed and personal form, have tried to show that while Poulenc in any one aspect of his art was not unusual, and sometimes even crassly derivative, when two or more aspects fused, sparks flew and life emerged. The Why is hard to focus on, creative vitality having no explication. But the What and the How are tangible. To recapitulate:

Although he is the most performed French vocal composer of his generation, the long-hewn spacious air is far less characteristic of Poulenc's melody than is the straightforward tune. (The straightforward tune, what's more, seems the happy medium of all French composers, except for those few whose outright impressionism renders them melodically devious. I exclude Ravel, who had it both ways, and Franck, who was from another century—and Belgian.) Yet even his tunes, as the years rolled on, grew elliptical, until in *Dialogues des Carmélites* and all ensuing vocal works, the sung line becomes almost wholly recitative. Nevertheless this line, in whatever medium and however digested, seems to be the signature of Poulenc—the added ingredient which makes any robbed recipe his.

Thus stolen harmonies—lost chords—like *objets trouvés* become a personal brand by dint of the tune that binds them. Thus an assemblage of simple counterpoints conspires to form chords which vertically sound like someone else's but whose moving top voice chants pure Poulenc. Thus his rhythms (which like his tunes are quintessentially French in their four-squareness), although humdrum in themselves, present solid planks on which to build his special tunes.

Those tunes, like Ives's, all sprang from the town-band dance-hall memories of youth, seen through a glass darkly. If it could be argued that an artist is one who retrieves unbroken the fragility of his past, or that a child is "the musician beforehand," then Poulenc, as glimpsed through the bittersweet contagion of his vocal phrases, is the child-artist incarnate.

Inasmuch as this paper was composed apropos of a revival of his religious opera, it has not seemed urgent to stress the sensual human. Another time I may write of how Poulenc (whose name, please, rhymes with tank) *became* his music while composing: how during the gestation of *Les Mamelles* he gaily cruised the boardwalk of Deauville, while during the birth pangs of *Dialogues* he developed stigmata and was confined to a Swiss clinic from where he wrote (premature) farewell letters. An essay could also be devoted to how his music became Poulenc: how all the more substantial works contain (oh, quite objectively) aspects of the composer's origins and tastes: the pell-mell elegant array of bourgeois and royalist and rough trade and holy water, of gourmand and esthete, pristine and maculate. If financial security (a fortune from Rhône-Poulenc pharmaceuticals) shaped his life, and therefore his music, a chaos of insecurity opened for those around him with his death. But I've said enough.

There are only a certain number of anecdotes, and I saw him only a certain number of times. When a catalogue is closed by death, when potential stops, survivors can only rediscuss forever the same works, revive the same tales, until those tales and works begin to swerve, to shift their weight and their meaning as we too narrow our interests and reevaluate in the light of advancing shadows. Next year I'll write another appraisal—perhaps with another slant—about this man whose memory and music I adore.

Part Four

Notes on Death

In *Paul's Case* the boy committing suicide witnesses his own dying, until suddenly the witnessing mechanism snaps off, and in blackness all returns to natural order. In childhood I identified with Paul, the oversensitive parvenu who, like Lily Bart, could no longer bear it. At the same time I sensed that Lily and Paul were unfit subjects for grown-up books. To read Cather and Wharton was to indulge a guilty luxury (luxury of vicarious suicide) when my mind, like Paul's and Lily's, should have been on important items like gym class or useful contacts. Adults, one assumed, put away childish things, broken hearts.

One can live and die by literary reference, not so much because one cannot distinguish fact from fiction as because fiction imposes itself forever upon fact, gives fact fragrance and shape, never permits fact to function in the abstract. Unless the very abstraction of fact is itself a fiction.

Could I be dead (rather than dying), given the indifferent motion of shadows emitting perfumes of ginger and formaldehyde? Dead nostrils don't inhale. Nor does dead gray matter recall the skill of a Janet Frame whose nonhero, pronounced moribund, nevertheless arose from an unguarded coffin to walk home, where a distraught but aquiescent mate was unable to accept him as viable, and in the end, years later, the neighbors stoned him to death for real.

Misdiagnosed as dead. Misdiagnosed as living.

To wait alone in the subway is said to be risky, although terms of risk change with the seasons. Criminals once were those sleazy folks who importuned in toilets; today those same evildoers become victims of desexualized muggers. Now during this midnight what will disturb the stillness? No shadow braids the low rows of girders, nothing forbodes. As in the Cordova mosque or Nantucket's graveyard I've never felt calmer.

Socrates' plea for an afterlife rests on the *donnée* of man's soul: the fact of the soul is as foregone a conclusion as the fact of the body. If there is no soul then all *Phaedo* collapses except as poetry. But perhaps there is only a soul, and no body.

Scene. During his suicidal preparation (loading pistol, lighting gas, shaking out Nembutal) the phone rings. A friend wants advice: on the stock market, on dealing with new junctures in love, on how to resolve a Neapolitan sixth. He gives the advice, lucidly, wittily, correctly. Then hangs up and kills himself.

Awash in his own blood he wonders: Is a work of art that from which one is safe? Is the poem a bridge to danger? (Danger to the poet, that is. For the public a poem is ever a bridge to safety.)

Does art succeed when it fails? A suicide that fails—leaving the victim alive and therefore an observer of his own "demise"—succeeds. Here I lie in my life's blood grinning, and am I my art? Who takes thus this *coup de théâtre*?

If to suffer from unrequited love is a waste of time, why should the documentation of that love—rendering it as history, as art—be time wisely spent? (Such practical queries! When in reality the world is unreal.)

The opposite of a hoarder of pieces of string, I need to clean out, throw away, empty ashtrays, spit. Once they were transcribed neatly, I used to incinerate notebooks and manuscripts, proud of my beautifully inked copy which served for eventual publication. Then I learned, for posterity and taxes, to keep all. It goes against nature, but today I clasp, ghoulishly wondering where now are those masses of deep-felt letters to JA, to Henri Fourtine, to Marie Laure, notes to dead lovers which when reread so come back to life (the lovers, not the letters).

Letters to myself, like this diary, I treasure but don't covet. A diary's an embarrassment we love, like a pet spaniel screwing a stranger's leg. Or old poems, like the "Sestina for Old Odors" from 1957. Is there a sestina by anyone that says anything, or even that works virtuosically? We speak of certain finished works as being deceptively easy. The sestina is deceptively complex—anyone can compose one on the spot with a semblance of meaning, although no sestina has meaning not more clearly stated in prose. (And no, this isn't true for all poetry.) Maybe music's the final home for the form. If it is a conceit to title a musical piece *Sonnet*, as Liszt did, it would not be so with *Sestina*. Music can't rhyme, but like a sestina it can have literal echoes, and even, should you want them, iambic meters.

For an autobiography a logical and legitimate scenario could be built from other people's letters, especially love letters. Who has the nerve for plunging into those tear-filled trunks? To spend too long there means life is past. Yet such letters make landmarks. Who was I, or who did I think I was, when X thirty years ago sent those unhappy words, or Y twenty years ago, or Z ten? Alone the memento box labeled "Marie Laure" provides a portrait of both her and me at a fixed point in French history.

Love letters are the food of retrospect, introspect, and extroversion. What about hate letters? And business letters?

Many of the greatest books have happy endings. *Middlemarch. A Room with a View.* Any others?

How is my actual death conceivable when my idea of death exists only in—indeed, was conceived only by—myself, never in you (even if you *are* Death), and must, so to speak, die with me?

When Camus claimed that the primal philosophical premise—the question to be settled before further discussion —was that of suicide, of whether life were worth living at all, he skipped a point. If life were not worth living, who would bother to discuss even that question? And surely those successful suicides, of sound mind and body, should be consulted after the fact. The first premise should be whether the question of suicide merits discussion. If it does, discuss it only after consulting the dead.

Thus the initial concern is not whether life's worth living but whether death's worth dying. When it kills, suicide fails. True success is to come back, to have your cake and eat it. Mishima's cake took the form of an international press release, yet he couldn't eat it since he lost his head. Still, like Marilyn, he acted out a universal dream by bidding goodbye before too late, at the height of power and beauty.

Suicide as an art form. Mishima at his peak dies publicly for what he feels to be truth. Truman Capote at the ebb of his power kills himself publicly for what he knows to be nontruth. Where Mishima grows ennobled, Capote shrivels (if a toad puffed up with hot air can be said to shrivel). His sketches of others are ultimately harmless, but the unwitting self-portrait is putrid as Dorian Gray's.

All that Truman touches turns to fool's gold. A book may or may not be a work of art, but it's not for the writer to say so, or even to know so. An artist doesn't "do art," he does work. If the work turns out as art, that's determined by others after the fact. Art and morality aside, Truman's work can't work. A work which names real names but whose author is fictitious? An author must be true, his characters fictitious.

Yes, the suicides that don't kill you are like keeping your cake. But an artist too has his cake and eats it. He suffers, but is appreciated for his suffering, and this very appreciation is an appeasement, a parole. Is the pain thus less intense, less aimless than an anonymous death in an internment camp? Does a rich person feel less ache, in the absolute, than a poor person with the same malady?

Art and unhappiness are unrelated. Because an artist sees the truth as a way out, and can do nothing, he is unhappy. Because he is seen seeing the way out, he is happy. And he often is willing to market his misery, sweep his madness onto a talk show and laugh at his own tears. Perhaps finally the greatest intelligence is an ability for joy. But joy in our land is equated with money. (It is a truth universally acknowledged that a single man in possession of a good fortune must be queer.)

Unhappy people are all alike; a happy person is happy in his own way. Every aphorism is reversible. Surely nothing's more monotone than misery, even the misery of philosophers and especially of lovers, whose individuality dissolves into uniform tears dampening their staunchest friendship. Unhappiness is a privilege of the young, the interresemblant young. But happy people are as unalike as snowflakes, though more . . . more elastic. Happiness, a prerogative of the wise, rejects nothing. Happiness cannot intrinsically lead to unhappiness any more than clarity comes of navel-gazing, but it can lead to ecstasy, even to death. Did not Olivier in *Les Faux Monnayeurs* declare that suicide alone was comprehensible after reaching such heights of joy that anything afterward must become a permanent letdown?

Is even suicide worth it? The small comfort of art. Art has even less "meaning" than life. Art does not outlast life. We've not the least notion of what Bach meant to Bach. Art salves loneliness perhaps, but is no cure for cancer.

Nausea at the news of a friend's death is balanced by guilty twinges of expectancy on turning to the obits: the disappointment when "nobody" today is commemorated. Yet for survivors each death brings the adventure of a new start. With one less acquaintance to distract them the road is cleared to fresh arrangements. The world's weight's changed. But soon these losses announce that they're just that, losses, potholes never to be filled, and those ever more numerous dead hail us with one moan that won't soften as it recedes, but grows more touching, ice clear, wished for, out of reach, adorable, tough.

To contend, as certain aging (and only aging, never young) people do, that sexual indifference to the elderly is discriminatory is logically to infer that avoidance of sex with children is discriminatory. Infantism. By extension necrophilia should not be discouraged. Well, perhaps it's rationalization, but if the young don't lust for the old there's simply not that much to lust for. I, for one, feel far less the need for proof, for making out, for taking the hours away from work that sex, any sex, requires.

The flesh stays willing, it's the spirit that's weak.

Nature designed us to be "attractive" from puberty to menopause, roughly thirty years. The gerontophilia so desired by older folks is, on the whole, bigoted: they resent not being loved by the young, but are sexually indifferent to their own age group.

Man, in meditating and in searching for God, does not transcend his human condition, he expands it. All that he does is, finally, human. Inhumanity, superhumanity are human concepts and have nothing to do with God.

God gave man his grand talents, the devil gave man his little ones—though the reverse could be convincingly reasoned. So-called responsible artists always talk about how they won't sell their soul for an easy buck. But their soul is precisely what buyers don't want. The soul is the one part of themselves they're allowed to keep when they reach Hollywood.

Have I an *oeuvre?* If I die tonight what single piece do I leave? No *Maldoror* surely, no *Four Saints* nor even *Little Foxes*—none of those works, like Shostakovich's First Symphony, penned young and shining. It's not for me to say that my output, like Chopin's or Janet Flanner's, is an assemblage, letters and preludes, nourishing one-page meals. Second day of the blizzard, alone in Nantucket with thumping radiators and the slumping basement, humanoid moans from a crack in the wall all night and if that stricture in my chest flings me floorward how long do I lie?

Was that heart ever wrapped in *Serenade* which this morning I finished and mailed to Ohio? Must heart always distinguish output? Distinguished output should *appear* to have heart. Our best work is not always what we feel deepest but what we work hardest on. This is most true for long-term results like operas or "functioning" marriages. (The joke is when something we work on hard also flops.) Pieces dashed off, but dashed off with heart and that succeed, are generally short, like songs.

More and more I receive requests (oh, not a constant flow, but every few months) to dredge up yesterday: souvenirs of the dance, of France *d'après-guerre*, of Paul Goodman and other recent dead. Less and less I care. My life has been based on my life. But isn't it wrong, morally wrong, to eat the past? When we die, our bodies and those shards of our vanity which served as precious bark should be forgotten, flung to feed poppies. Why, then, do I trouble to note this? From habit, it's all I know.

As I lay dying, might the final page of Josquin's *Missa Pange Lingua* help to waft me off? No, death doesn't busy itself with "fine" emotions. Death is disgusting. Nor does death approach, no matter how expected or even desired, with what we call taste. *J'ai médité sur la mort chaque heure de ma vie, et cela maintenant ne me sert de rien!* Thus intoned Poulenc's Prieur from the stage of the Salle Garnier on June 21, 1957, and every hour since then I've mulled those words. Were the Prieur's disciplined fancies finally so far from mine? That as we sink into the winding sheet those sunny others leave for a party to which we're not invited? (Why say *we*? Nothing is less *we* than dying. A priest is no help as he leads you to the gallows.)

Write the tale of a man who all his life dreads death, but who on his deathbed realizes the waste, for death is not dreadful at all.

In Hyères, April 1951, Félix Labisse offered to Marie Laure a housegift in the form of a canny little illustrated tome named *Le Livre du Suicide*. Certain morbid types among the *sous bourgeoisie* commit suicide ornately according to execution methods of their homeland. Thus in Vanves the fat local butcher and father of seven, after donning a gold wig and fluffy tutu, managed to behead himself with an axblade lashed to the base of a two-ton armoire.

By 1954 I had not only confected a libretto loosely based on Stevenson's *Suicide Club* (which I called *The Dying Room* in homage to Graham Greene's current play *The Living Room*), but actually completed a few airs and trios before shelving the deal as a dull bargain.

I picture everything dead. Over the day I picture the cat, the checkout girl at the A&P, that usher. The melancholy is elusive, not in definition but in whereabouts. I chase after melancholy, desirous, sliding around corners. Later it arrives in this room uncalled-for. Certain things we'll comprehend only after we're gone. The time from now till then visibly shrinks like the *peau de chagrin* and brings a faint smile.

As a figment of my own imagination do I fake insanity when sane? Or fake sanity when mad? The Great Man's key is less genius than patience. It's not that Balzac was actually smarter than real people; he had a compulsive discipline. Though by that definition any long-winded enthusiast for whom a guitar looms larger than Priapus is a magician.

That I should be omitted from so trivial an exchange is hardly insulting, yet I'd have preferred the omission to be acknowledged. My presence is not ignored so much as seen through, as through a glass dazzlingly, or as one swims while paying the water no heed. No one mentions my epitaph, or even drops my name. Are ghosts aware of themselves? Can they ask themselves that question?

Yaddo. This noon in the thick rain I carried my lunch pail over to Elizabeth's little house and we sat together for two hours there. Mostly she talked about the vast wedding last month of Marianne, and I was shown the gorgeous bridal gown in the cedar chest upstairs. But maybe, too, she spoke on other things, I can't remember. Because as I nibbled raw carrots and wild cherries all concentration was for Elizabeth's right eyelid. Upon it already a year ago there appeared a noticeable darkening, a sort of bruised lump; today it has spread and festered, is redder, oozing. My hostess made no allusion to it nor did I, but as we chattered on, swallowing and bemoaning, I grew hypnotized by that wound, which took on its own life, while Elizabeth's words seemed as remote to me as mine (in her deafness) must always seem to her. Can it be cancer? The smear now swelled to the size of a rotted apricot, extended feelers, and began crawling down her right cheek. Elizabeth, I no longer wish to discuss my own problems, but the Artist's, it all comes to the same but with more generous phrasing. The taut skin throbbed like a timpani, and though the left side of her head remained normal, the whole right side became a pineapple melting onto the lace of her shoulder, and finally into her lap, a sheet of soft taffy in which the running eye was located at about the level of her breast. Yes, she agreed that an objectifying of my concerns is indicated at this time if only I could learn, as she has, to enjoy being alone, compose not for someone but for everyone, and smell the petunias. Indeed, the petunias' rich odor was rampant everywhere, it having been pouring since 3 A.M. when I awoke to the thundering on the tin roof and never returned to sleep but lay entertaining vital clarifications which only, it appears, appear unusually. I was exhausted now, poured myself another cup of skim milk while Elizabeth continued her never unnecessary speaking. The river of her eye's infection had reached the floor, gushing rapidly now, and hairily made its way toward me. Had I met Wallace Fowlie yet? Well yes, and liked him more than I had anticipated. I could do without Yaddo's surplus of mosquitoes and deerflies, but could do *with* a haircut, it's longer than ever in my life, really quite mod. My feet were embalmed in mud, I stood up quickly. Elizabeth! I yelled, there's a tree blossoming on your path outside: show it to me, because I must go to work now and the rain's stopped. We walked a few paces together toward the locust tree, enchanted and hung with wet crystals. The sky was clearing ever so slowly. Elizabeth looked well for her unknown age and sprightly, but said she needs rest. So we murmured goodbye, until tonight.

(She explains that her eye condition results from a beautician's accident some forty years ago. A white-hot curling iron glanced her cornea, permanently destroying the oil glands, or something.)

All is habit, and so is art. Death is the giving up of our last and hardest habit, life. Life is a rehearsal of death. But at the final curtain, the very pain of agony helps to mask the coming horror.

Eyes and eggs make potatoes and turkeys, and turkeys and potatoes make eggs and eyes. So rolls the hoop forever. Humankind too, reproducing itself, comes up with endlessly undifferentiated models. Only a work of art—even a bad one—grows from a seed toward a singular finish and writes a unique Stop.

JH contends that whereas Virgil's prose is to instruct, mine is to punish.

Instruction and punishment are two sides of one coin (the third side is satire). What we call Life is the scattered attempt to get even with those who "misunderstood" us in childhood. What we call Art is the disciplined attempt to get even.

It's been four years since I've smoked, five since I've drunk, and six since I first met JH. Has this abstinence (which viewed differently might be named indulgence) recolored me? I no longer get depressed. Saddened, yes, by the reality of a dying planet, but not overcome as with hangovers by my own willfully damaged body. Death's real, but dwelling on death is not.

Letter this morning from Christiane Fourtine in Cugnaux. Henri is dead. He died, in fact, four months ago, before my trip to Paris last spring, and after a year of torture from intestinal cancer. In her second sentence Christiane (whom

I met only once, years ago, and found to be a shy farm girl)
affirms that she tended her husband day and night despite
the meanness and neglect he had shown her through their
conjugal life. *"C'est seulement dans le malheur,"* she goes
on, *"qu'il a compris qu'un foyer était plus précieux et surtout
plus solide que les amis de rencontre."*

Les amis de rencontre. But I was one of them. Indeed, we
were, each of us, that life-changing chance encounter which
took place in an April dusk of 1952 near the Observatoire
garden. *"Un café, ça vous dit?"*, he had said. I recall each
phrase of our ensuing night in the Hôtel des Saints-Pères, of
the next weeks, the next two years, the very very intense
odoriferous sex, the thorough snarling satisfaction that has
since not been equaled, not certainly in America.

So now he's dead, the paragon. And every shred of that
liveliness (the only body which could make my body lose its
head) lies decomposing underground. Today it's too easy
to write I'd felt it; yet his silence of the last two years made
me suspect that Henri was unwell, more indeed than his
wife and children of whose maladies he'd written me. It is
extraordinary how we allow people to come and go in our
hearts and heads, how we reanimate at will the quick and
dead, oceans away. Each morning begins the numbing wait
till night. The sole preoccupation is: How will these days
complete themselves. As an adolescent with Maggy in those
West Chicago bars I ruminated that there we were, in the
small packed room as in a trap, but a trap that was life and
not death, for outside lurked the empty streets, behind them
the prairie, and beyond the prairie death, closing in, gradual
but sure, and all this glued onto a sphere hurtling dumbly
across the sky.

Christiane solicits nothing. She must (she writes) spend
the rest of her life providing for the youngsters with her

limited resources. Her note exudes no sorrow. Yet how can I know? My Henri was the dessert, she had the main course. With no sense whatsoever of responsibility I keep him alive at leisure here in the flame of this room. These ever more frequent black-rimmed announcements make me bristle more than weep. They contain a certain *mauvais goût*.

With each friend that dies some of me dies. I am bereft, not because that part of me which he embodied is lost, but because that part of him which I embodied is lost. He can no longer impart to others his version of myself.

Rereading the famous conversation (in Herodotus, and again in Plutarch) between Croesus and Solon, the premise seems cantish. Happiness, like love, is at best impermanent for intelligent people, and should be defined solely in terms of the moment, not in terms of longevity. Cannot a man *have been* happy (we might ask Solon) although he's not happy now? Croesus with all his riches did fall, but he also rose again.

"Just one minute more: I was about to understand everything." These are the words which Valéry once said he would say on his deathbed. They go Madame Du Barry one better.

Although we've corresponded lately because of the piece Tommy Schippers is commissioning for the Cincinnati Symphony, it's been years since our last meeting. His beauteous wife has died and he himself has just undergone surgery for a spastic esophagus, while I've passed through a critical birthday and am for the moment a hobbling cripple. Thus when I step from the elevator and into his more-than-comfortable lodgings at 550 Park we appraise each other warily. Tommy in a sky-blue sweater and white slacks remains young and handsome but drawn and pained, and I feel a concerted effort on his part during our three-hour tête-à-tête.

Twenty-two years since we first shook hands in the Bar Montana, rue St.-Benoît. How different those years have been for each of us. How different indeed are the various categories of musician who to the outsider appear all the same. Conductor and composer, doer and maker, are in fact as disparate in professional duty and personal habit as gardener and botanist. Tommy's career has been all public and lavish, concentrated labor on other people's music, and a marriage, which he describes as idyllic, which resolved in sadness. That he should wish me to compose for his orchestra comes as a happy surprise, since his only (public) reaction to my music has been hitherto adverse.

Although the weather is pure spring, the sun was setting already when we parted at four. Despite his fame and fortune Tommy seems an orphan now cursed for his blessings by the gods.

The "objectivity" of Paul's suicide—his seeing it happen while it happened, his *using* it—didn't make it any less doleful than did, for instance, my tantrums in adolescence, refusing to eat, while noting coolly that the diet trimmed down my figure.

Cocktails at Gethsemane. Peter named Paul, this is Paul named Peter. May we introduce you both to Percy named Mae. And here comes Ebenezer named Archibald along with George called Myrt. But where's Elsa named Charles? and Joan called John?

With no special pang, suddenly I realize there's no longer regular contact with a single person in Europe. Paris has become like Chicago, a city which once was the world, my sole frame of reference, a globe now withering, receding. It takes a telescope to find it. Finding myself in France tonight I'd be at a loss as to whom to phone.

Deciannual visit from Dick Jacob sporting the identical features as in our Chicago adolescence. Conversation nine-tenths reminiscence. I recall that Don Dalton first introduced us to the voice of Billie Holiday in 1939. Dick grows indignant about Don (dead for three decades) for he had given Don that disk, yet Don took credit for presenting "Fine and Mellow" to South Side's intelligentsia. Similarly today I still nurse grudges against poor Bill Flanagan, who defends himself even less well than when he was alive. This is not especially unhealthy.

The trouble with pornography is no viewpoint. It's not more honest than. It's only simpler than. Blue blue blue blue blue, the Manhattan air takes on airs of whory sentience to beguile us as we prepare to leave for months.

Auden says: Those who hate to go to bed fear death, those who hate to get up fear life.

Aren't these analogies identical? And isn't Auden anyway wrong? Children hate to go to bed, and they aren't conditioned to forebodings good or bad. It's rather a question of halting inertia, altering an aspect of life (for in life there is no death, not even dying is death). I, for one, enjoy waking up and enjoy going to sleep. Dreamland is not a void but a vital geography.

Three weeks ago Alvin Ross came to dine and described his recent barium (which proved ultimately to show a malignancy). Stretched on his back, he was able to watch on a ceiling screen the X rays filtering through his intestine. The two interns paused, their heads converged to a point on the film, silence reigned as Alvin, too, focused on what looked like a wee embryo moving hazily in a pond—a deep pool within his body and simultaneously there above him. Since that night—by sympathy, coincidence, antipathy?—I too am prey. This morning Alvin enters Beth Israel.

To be aware of your own death. Everyone else goes on to dumb festivities, while you stay home alone and die. To say this means in some way to care—that I'm not incapacitated. Yet I've said all I have to say. In which case, such a final saying seems . . . Long nights.

Most of the time I feel lousy. Unable to underplay, I recount my own misery. Why? It's not a pleasure to wonder how I'll kill myself; suicide's not child's play, nor can anyone accept, even for a moment, Freud's verses anymore. ("No man can believe in his own death. And when he tries to imagine it, he perceives that he really survives as a spectator.") Were it not for JH where would I be? The drift of a high-school lass's diary comes back to haunt us.

Back in New York to find Jay Harrison nailed in a coffin. Deaths which "don't come as a surprise" surprise us most. Being expected, we write them off before they occur. When they occur we're doubly grieved. No gulf is wider than between the almost dead and the dead.

Deaths today of Marcel Achard and of Harry Partch, the arrière-garde of France and the avant-garde of America. Why are we less attracted to a contemporary artist's work after he dies? When friends die the excruciation is that we'll never see them again. That "never" is what leaves me cold when artists pass away—artists, that is, who aren't particularly friends. That their catalogue is now complete lames rather than quickens interest.

Everything has ego. Not just cats and plants and that bowl of tortoise eggs, but a pile of pillows, a steel bed, radiators exist there, without moving, ominous, taking up your space. I am not nice. Pretend to be, even try to be. But I'm not. Also I'm dull, though having learned to feign sparkle, I get along.

Weary and without illusion, I persist in noting it. Why even write? Why even write "Why even write 'Why even write' "Why even write" ' "?

If you know you are going to die, if you're condemned and the date is set, nothing—no creed or philosophy, no friendly phrase or stoical recipe—makes any difference. The fact of your near and certain end becomes as all-consuming as love was years ago.

Visit from Robert Veyron-Lacroix, here on his annual trek with Rampal. We gave him boned chicken breasts marinated in ale and garlic, baked yams, a watercress salad, and strawberry mousse with framboise-flavored raspberry sauce.

Since we meet so seldom our rapports cannot center on the present. We know to some extent what we have become, while the past evanesces increasingly. I was interested in whether Roro had ever returned to Hyères. Yes, two years ago, having to play in Toulon, he detoured bravely to the Chateau St. Bernard. Henri, the caretaker, who now lives alone over the garage, warned Roro that the property would seem a *triste* shock. The once-manicured lawns are yards high in weeds, vines have grown through the windows and rend the concrete floors. The fifty-room house, once filled with Kislings and pianos, esprit and quarrels, hard work and gold wealth, is now an empty station with a cold wind. Roro said it was ugly (that it always had been, but we never noticed), and has been sold to the town to be converted, like Edith Wharton's mansion nearby, into an inn. So there it is, where my only songs for eight years saw the light, every cranny familiar as my pocket, dust now, like her.

I'm now doing what everyone only plans to do: reading Proust from start to finish simultaneously in French and English. I had read *Swann's Way* twice in the forties, but found it unhandy to complete during a decade in France. The reason: Marie Laure (whose grandmother Chevigné served as model for the Duchesse de Guermantes) always found him a *vieux raseur*, never read him, and didn't comprehend until his death what she'd missed—although as a toddler she had been dandled on Proust's knee and in the ensuing years had had ample access to the author. Result: she denied the very fact of Proust, banished his books, and told me to read more urgent writers for my French education. Like Quéneau.

His work is alien to those mighty fanciful flights of other sociologists—a Petronius or a Henry James. His famous asides notwithstanding, the earmark is one-track-mindedness. He eschews poverty, alcoholicism, menu specifics, physical cruelty, religion and details of sexual acts (except the few unconvincing scenes in Jupien's hotel with their farcical coincidences, tough talk, stereotype perversions. An old-fashioned whip of nails is not a torture when the "victim" craves it). Proust describes what is. His milieu is no less familiar to Americans than Melville's to Frenchmen, and, as Paul Goodman never tired of saying (the obvious always digs deepest), "One thing leads to another," which Proust knew well, and Proust knew all.

Is it heresy to suggest that he was not homosexual? Insofar as he was sexual at all, Proust's vicariousness is slanted straight. Marcel's conclusions on homosexuality, even when drowsing in the predawn of our current awakening, are just too touristy. Charlus, that lovable contemporary of Wilde and precursor of Djuna Barnes's doctor, is a marvel when being a learned snob, but a joke when being a fractious fruit. Proust's notion, like that of puritan grade-school principals, is that sodomites are all in a continual state of cruising, that's their defining characteristic, and that even the most cultured of lesbians (like Bloch's sister) will, when left to their own devices, perform cunnilingus in hotel lobbies.

As for Moncrieff, someone sometime must surely write an essay on his famous job. Translation is the wrong word. It's hideously magnificent and has something to do with Proust. Yet, if it has little to do with French, it has a lot to do with English. Any fool can see that *Sodome et Gomorrhe* translates as *Sodom and Gomorrah*, not as *Cities of the Plain*. But if this bowdlerization could be explained by the pristine censors of yore, why retitle the unoffending *Albertine disparue* as *The Sweet Cheat Gone?* As for gay jargon, Moncrieff did use the word "camp" way back then, an exquisite find for what lacked in the original, though elsewhere he merely misleads us by transliterating Jupien's reference to Charlus' cock—*Vous en avez un gros pétard!*— as "Aren't you naughty!" and he quite miffs us by calling a *raseur* a "shaver," whatever that may be.

Will anyone deny that Moncrieff's is not a commendable Life's Work in its own right?

Blossom errs. His ear is tin, his balance rickety. One example will do. For the last word Proust reserved the crucial *temps*. To intensify its impact he understandably avoided that word for several previous paragraphs. Blossom sees fit (lest we miss the point?) to inject Time (capitalized) thrice within the final sentence, so that *his* last word falls flat.

Why is Nantucket unsexy? For the same reason, in a sense, that Proust isn't sexy. People here are too well off. All consideration for tastes of coloring and nationality aside, sexiness comes from the financially underprivileged. The rich don't *need* to be sexy. Any Greek waiter or *ragazzo di vita* exudes more carnality than the handsomest duke in town. And if the northern peoples are less sexy than the Mediterranean it's because they are by nature more privileged, that is, by dint of the preserving cold they are less prey to decay: Northerners are inherently permanent, while sexiness is transient. I'm speaking, of course, strictly for the male sex. A beautiful woman, no matter how wealthy, is still underprivileged and by that token sexual.

There are those who thrill at the idea of a Visconti movie, *In Search of Lost Time*, and the prospect of Brando as Charlus. Neither the Absolute General nor the Absolute Particular has ever been filmed convincingly. Kafka's *Trial* is an instance of Absolute General, K. being Everyman—that is, ourself—and thus a Tony Perkins can only outrage our personal fantasy. *In Search of Lost Time* is an instance of Absolute Particular, Marcel being Oneman—that is, Narrator Proust—and thus Visconti's vision can only jar *our* vision of Proust's vision. A ballet perhaps? But Proust is nothing if not French, while Brando, whatever his breadth, is nothing if not American, and oh, the common gratuitous assumption (by an Italian) that American names might depict the exquisite wit of milieux now nearly unremembered even by rich elderly Parisians.

Place de la Madeleine. Given what finally emerged, could one claim that the potential was contained in the madeleine when first tasted? Can a man be potentially an artist (or a dreamer of the past) if he never realizes himself as an artist (or a dreamer)? If the future is contained, literally contained, in the present, supposing a man dies before the future (the eating of the second madeleine) arrives? What becomes of this nipped-in-the-bud future? The world existed in that madeleine not in fact but because Marcel said it did. (Interesting that in an earlier draft his madeleine was toast.)

Unrequited love, mystery of the common cold, hate for a person who's forgotten us, the women's vote, a crossword puzzle. Solutions often come from unexpected sources. Dazzled by the pearly gates we miss the trapdoor.

Awakened as usual by the predawn gurgle of pigeons on the sill, satisfying tones which swell, melt, dissolve, fade like an aerial shot of Niagara. A loud sloppy flutter, silence again, flush of a far toilet, then a din of traffic starts to grow. Do birds dream? Gulf of insomnia, so all-important during the endless uninteresting minutes, yet so insignificant in retrospect. With luck I'll drift off, but at 8:50 sharp Wallace pads into the room with a no-nonsense *meow!* which officially starts the day.

The life I lived was the life I lived; how could I have known it was history? History—who says? Could not the gardener—if not in name at least in shame or glory—have been fixed there too? If he *is* fixed there in my reverie, does he vanish with my death, though I remain fixed (fixed?) in notes and nouns?

October 23rd. So I am fifty-two, the age at which Shakespeare, on his birthday, died. Birthday of Sarah Bernhardt, Johnny Carson, Franz Liszt, Miriam Gideon, Maurice Grosser.

Marre de la mort, marre des arbres qui ne rendent pas leur secret, marre de la mauvaise critique pour ce que j'exerce—quoique borné—mieux que quiquonque. Sick of death, sick of trees which don't tell their secret, sick of bad reviews for what I practice—however restricted—better than anyone.

To emerge from the sadness of late youth into the smugness of early middle age was to declare that, barring bad health, unhappiness was unseemly after forty. Today it remains unseemly (and ever so boring to outsiders), while becoming the sole logical stance. But keep it quiet, if you can, and stick to your faithful Quaker guns.

Pale hand aquiver on the receiver (for it's anxious-making to phone even close friends, let alone comparative strangers, especially ones we admire) I waited for five rings after which, when he did answer, it was clear I'd wakened him, though it was noon. "Shall I call back later—at two, say?" "Well, I've a tentative lunch appointment, make it after" —but no hint that *he* call *me*, though his tone was friendly enough, and he had suggested we meet when I returned to town. (The only time we did meet, eight years ago, he'd not made it easy either, with that deceptive warm way teachers have of obliging students to make the first pass.) Well, now it's six o'clock, I won't call back, how can I? Let history determine what's been missed.

Maybe there's not always need to meet those we respect. A man's conversation can't always equal, in clarity and condensation, what he's written. But Martin Duberman did earn my admiration, if only because of his public penitence for the awful review he gave, years ago, to Paul Goodman's masterpiece, *Five Years*.

Sometimes I wonder if M's disease has caught up to me, when smell of a cooked carrot or sight of a mere vase brings on tears.

If my oft-uttered contention holds—that we don't change, we just get more so—then I've always been a crank, even when most *mignon*, and it shows increasingly through rancor and envy which I take out on patient friends, ever fewer. In the cold street those nonlooks we sling at long-lost contemporaries counteract keenly the gentle cruising we once ... oh, we pretend not to see each other, for there now without the grace of God go I. All those missed opportunities (exclusively carnal) from drinking too much become missed opportunities from not drinking at all; shyness and logic (which aren't the same) preclude stumbling into the barren boredom of prescrewing chitchat. Last night I began finally *Elle et Lui* (phrase by which Henri Hell and his boyfriend once were known) thanks to the lamentable TV series "Notorious Woman." It's about having the time to miss opportunities, and at least rich Sand could impose rules better than thin Rosemary Harris, who, thanks to a sterile director and a bromidic script, turns narrow, super-American, sans class, and terribly petty. Sand was nothing if not

French, had style, scope, talent. She knew how to enter rooms.

Felicia Bernstein's birthday. The invitation promises cocktails at eight, dinner at nine. Shaved and shining I arrive at the Lotos Club promptly, then grow queasy at that massive stone, that menacing Rolls, that showbiz luxe, and can't bring myself to go in. Two hours later I return, ashamed, and actually check my coat in the foyer. Yet the thought of effecting a lone ascent by that curling stair toward the jolly tinkle and thick scents above so petrifies me that, for the second time, I retreat. Had I been with someone, no problem. But to enter anywhere alone (except onto a stage where the plan is aloof, formal, prepaid) intimidates me to where I get a headache that lasts for days.

Durability as proof? Baseball bats are more durable than cloisonné vases, sacks of potatoes than baked Alaskas, and Merv Griffin has survived Ned Rorem.

Ten years ago the fatal premiere of *Miss Julie*. Could I do better tonight? Differently, surely, and time flies fast. Works of art, said Proust, are less disappointing than life, for they do not begin by giving us the best of themselves. Yet are not various great works for me now exhausted (some by Stravinsky, for example, which once drained us repeatedly while retaining their own vitality, movements of Mozart, or Rembrandt or of Proust himself), while "life"—indeed the very "affair" with JH—is in continual flowering with the "best" yet to come, or how go on? Nets were finally flung and for some months there's been proximity of death. I am his host for he inhabits me, and his guest since he's provisionally placed me in a transparent placenta sack which, rather sooner than later, he'll rip open to the world's air, like a gas chamber's. Meanwhile he parades me about, a corpse on parole, chuckling as I balk at meager deadlines, write tunes, but easily distracted by television's lure. Death's female to the French. West Chester Street. Is this a street or some ancient thoroughfare through cemeteries which now, with daylight saving rescinded, turn blue by 4 P.M.? Alone on this island where I know no one, own a house, plain but costly, for the first time ever like grown-ups, and each evening after supper of lentils and Jello, take a constitutional through the seasonal mist down Lily Street encountering not a soul, and return to the dubious welcome thirty minutes later of Wallace the cat. Like ghosts of Hammerfest or Thule, Nantucket is far from anywhere, from America, from even a memory of childhood, though not from plagues that could accompany us to Mars, not from masculine death who glides at any speed. Why Nantucket? Why, when I've never owned a thing, buy a house in this Huguenot anti-art cranberry bog rather than in beloved Provence?

Allergic not just to seed and perfume, but to the smell of dollar bills and newsprint, Kleenex, water and thoughts of horses wild. JH tries to cope with my inability myself to cope. I fall apart, suffocate, scream. It's easy to write this now—but just one hour ago I saw *him*, NR, in flames, and JH at sea.

Yet there are moments every few days in Nantucket—during a flash of light across the page, during an afternoon pause in the Quaker cemetery—moments filled with happiness so clean you'd think they sprang from paradise. But in retrospect, sometimes as soon as one hour after, these moments seem unbearably sad. Is it because such moments, experienced only when alone, are remorse from the comparative passivity of contentment, even the contentment of the intellect at work, in arguments with JH or of trying a new recipe? No, the shock of happiness is so positive it resembles an invasion, burning energy with such speed that the recipient is left flat or, sometimes, dead.

Anyone can close the eyes of the dead, but who can open the eyes of the living?

How much time is left? Will the end hurt?

With Herbert Machiz' dying, the hill grows higher. In *War Scenes:* "The whole world, North and South, seemed one vast hospital. . . ." Herbert, the only artist with whom collaboration wasn't friction. I recall pleasurably the four or five plays we musicalized together. But what purpose is served by the death of friends, the ever grander bunch of bones? The same purpose as their living? Are skulls ground into a fertile dust?

Success doesn't make one less cranky, it lends authority to crankiness. As people age and turn more successful—or less successful—they tend to get more central. Tastes don't alter much, but viewpoint softens. Conservatives notoriously grow more liberal, radicals more conventional. In politics this is most visible, but in the arts too. Exceptions like Duchamp or Bertrand Russell only emphasize rules like Gertrude Stein, Stravinsky, Elliott Carter, Schoenberg, who all, it could be argued, evolved in the reverse.

Prizes and praise replace sex. Or rather, they are sex. Any number of public performers, while playing the so-called Serious Masterpieces, reach states of literal orgasmic trance.

Confession for the new year. My growing laziness (and this applies to general life as well as to this special paragraph

—its style and content and dubious desire for being) stems from knowing I've uttered all that's in me in as many accents as can be counterfeited. In the half-million words published, and in the thirty-plus hours of music composed, I've probably said most of what I know. Does there remain only to say it all again differently? Were they to announce "You will stay known and loved, and need never express yourself again; you will be rich and admired, but will never more compose"—would I feel deprived or relieved?

Having writ this, having professed forever that I can't know how the quality of my nice music or mean prose would hold were they not interdependent, I now believe they wound each other. To write words is finally very bad for my music.

Why persist? When we were children, Mother's father, Granddaddy Miller in Yankton, taught us all to knit—everything except how to cast off. That scarf was luscious, longer day by day, every week, month upon month, a woolen snake of many colors, I couldn't stop. There it still is over there, ivory needles still caught in those forty feet of indecision, its option, and only Isadora could have put an end to it.

Cynthia Ozick, Zionist, on learning that as a Quaker I was conditioned to think all war wrong while granting that certain Arabs have a point, poses the old canard: What if you're being mugged? Isn't that argument's fallacy now clear to all? Person-to-person is not people-to-people. (Lytton Strachey, asked what he'd do if a soldier were raping his sister, answered: "I'd try to get between them.") In theory Quakers turn the other cheek to muggers, and in fact police advise us to play dead. The question is not how Quakers feel about being mugged but how they feel about muggers. They aren't geared to protect themselves so much as to protect aggressors from themselves—to discourage need for war rather than assuming war as solution.

Earth is round, the trinity is round, the concept of the universe is eternally round. Yet although we dine from round plates we humans set those plates on rectangular tables on rectangular floors in rectangular houses on streets and acres and miles, all square. We paint pictures in angled frames and hang them in rooms that are never globes. Does the free animal perceive his world, his human friends, as spheres? Do we contradict possibilities of endless joy by blocking out our life? Could we curve our lives?

Galloping insomnia. Patches of wakefulness, ever larger, form a totally unraveled sleave. Can't recall not having been conscious.

Index